beginners
simple meals

step-by-step to perfect results

THE AUSTRALIAN
Women's Weekly

contents

Making dinner from scratch is easier than you think... and the recipes I've chosen for this book will prove it! Don't be afraid of cooking for others: homemade food cooked with enthusiasm and served with ease is within everyone's grasp. These recipes – straightforward yet tempting, healthy yet scrumptious, uncomplicated but special – will reward you with the kind of food we all want to cook (and eat!) today.

Pamela Clark

Food Director

Cut capsicum in half lengthways

Remove and discard seeds and membrane

Slice capsicum pieces thinly lengthways

crispy noodle salad

PREPARATION TIME **15 minutes**

SERVES 4

*Crispy fried noodles are sold packaged (usually in a 100g packet), already deep-fried and ready to eat.
They are sometimes labelled crunchy noodles, and are available in two widths – thin and spaghetti-like or
wide and flat, like fettuccine; we used the thin variety in this recipe.*

1 medium red capsicum (200g)

100g baby curly endive

100g crispy fried noodles

1 small red onion (100g), sliced thinly

1 tablespoon coarsely chopped fresh mint

**1 tablespoon coarsely chopped
 fresh coriander**

dressing

1/3 cup (80ml) peanut oil

1 tablespoon white vinegar

1 tablespoon brown sugar

1 tablespoon light soy sauce

1 teaspoon sesame oil

1 clove garlic, crushed

1 Cut capsicum in half lengthways. Remove and discard seeds and membranes; slice capsicum pieces thinly. Trim endive; discard hard ends of leaves.

2 Combine capsicum and endive with noodles, onion, mint and coriander in large bowl. Add dressing; toss to combine.

dressing Combine ingredients in a glass screw-top jar; shake well.

per serving 22.7g fat; 1104kJ

TIPS

● Have all the ingredients for this salad chopped and ready to go so that they can be tossed together with the dressing just before serving; the noodles become unappetising and soggy if the salad sits for any length of time.

● You can use any number of greens other than the baby curly endive: baby spinach, mizuna, coral or oak-leaf lettuce or even radicchio.

SERVING SUGGESTION
The subtle Asian flavours of this salad
are a fitting start to a main course of either
Salt and Pepper Chicken Skewers (page 29)
or Slow-Roasted Ocean Trout (page 77),
both of which are best accompanied by
steamed jasmine rice.

SERVING SUGGESTION

Accompany this soup with a basket of
warmed flour tortillas then follow it with
Chicken Enchiladas with Corn Salsa (page 18).
A platter of sliced, chilled assorted tropical fruits
is the perfect end to this Mexican-style meal.

Slow-roasted tomatoes give this soup an almost sweet "real" tomato flavour

Process the tomato mixture right in the pan in which it's been cooked, using a stab mixer

Rolling basil leaves into a tight cigar shape then slicing finely is called a chiffonnade

roasted tomato soup

PREPARATION TIME **15 minutes** ● COOKING TIME **1 hour**

SERVES 4

20 large egg tomatoes (1.8kg), quartered

2 tablespoons olive oil

2 cloves garlic, crushed

1 tablespoon balsamic vinegar

1/3 cup (80g) sour cream

2 tablespoons finely shredded fresh basil

1 Preheat oven to moderately slow.

2 Combine tomato, oil, garlic and vinegar in large baking dish; roast, uncovered, in moderately slow oven about 50 minutes or until soft.

3 Blend or process tomato mixture, in batches, until almost smooth. Transfer mixture to large saucepan; simmer, uncovered, until heated through.

4 Divide soup among serving bowls; top each portion with equal amounts of sour cream and basil.

per serving 17.5g fat; 910kJ

TIPS

● If possible, make this soup the day before you intend to serve it to allow the flavours to meld.
● You can use any kind of tomatoes but make certain they're not too soft; if they're overripe, they'll crush into a pulpy mass when you try to quarter them. And, since the olive oil is actually an important ingredient in this recipe, it's an ideal time to use a good-quality extra virgin olive oil – you'll definitely notice the difference in the taste of the soup.

● Peel the tomatoes before roasting to guarantee a super-smooth finish to the soup: core each tomato then cut a shallow cross in its base. Place tomatoes in a large heatproof bowl; cover with boiling water. Stand about 2 minutes before peeling away skin, from cross end toward top. If you can't be bothered peeling tomatoes but want a fine-textured soup, after you process the roasted tomato mixture, pass it through a fine sieve or a food mill (mouli) to catch the skins.

● Use a stab mixer, if you own one, to blend the tomato mixture when it's in the saucepan.
● Cutting the basil leaves in a chiffonnade (which translates from French as "made from rags" but in cooking refers to vegetables or herbs that have been cut into thin ribbons) is a beautiful way to present them. Stack several leaves then roll the stack like a cigar. Using a sharp knife, cut across the "cigar's" vein in as thin a slice as you can manage; separate the slices into perfect miniature squiggles of basil.

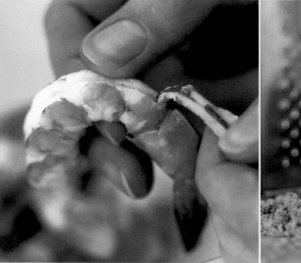

To shell prawns, grip the tail shell gently then pull off the body shell and legs; discard these – leaving the tail intact is primarily for appearance

After shelling, make a shallow incision down the back and scrape away the dark intestinal tract (this is called deveining); you can also use your fingers to pull out the vein

Grate the rind of the unjuiced lime without scraping off any of the bitter white layer, called the pith; both extra rind and juice can be frozen, separately, for another use

prawn cocktail with lime aioli

PREPARATION TIME **20 minutes**

SERVES 4

A modern take on the traditional prawn cocktail, this version uses baby rocket leaves rather than iceberg lettuce and replaces bottled cocktail sauce with aioli, a light and zesty garlic and lime mayonnaise.

40 medium cooked prawns (1kg)

100g baby rocket leaves

1/2 cup (150g) mayonnaise

2 teaspoons finely grated lime rind

2 tablespoons lime juice

2 cloves garlic, crushed

1 red thai chilli, seeded, sliced thinly

1 Shell and devein prawns, leaving tails intact.

2 Toss prawns with rocket in large bowl; divide among serving dishes.

3 Combine mayonnaise, rind, juice, garlic and chilli in small bowl; spoon evenly over prawns and rocket.

per serving 13g fat; 1078kJ

TIPS

● You can assemble the aioli early on the day you intend to serve it and refrigerate, covered. Similarly, if you shell and devein the prawns and store them in a small glass bowl, covered, in the refrigerator early on the day, then it's just a simple matter of tossing them with the rocket and dolloping on the aioli at mealtime.

● Always buy cooked prawns in the shell to guarantee that they have not lost their natural moisture and flavour. To shell prawns, grip the tail shell gently, then pull off the body shell and legs; discard these. Leaving the tail intact is mainly for appearance.

● Aioli is a Provençal garlic mayonnaise that's often used as a sauce for seafood and shellfish dishes; it's also perfect served with steamed vegetables, especially potatoes.

● Any of the many different lettuces so readily available today can be used instead of baby rocket. Choose one simply for its looks if you like: curly coral lettuce or red mignonette would look splendid in a glass with the prawns.

SERVING SUGGESTION
Serve, with fresh lime wedges and thinly sliced chilli, as the appetiser before our Tarragon Chicken and Leek Pies (page 21) or Lemon Veal Steaks with Broad Bean Mash (page 58).

SERVING SUGGESTION
Serve this salad before the Beef Ragù with Grilled Polenta (page 41)
for a contemporary Italian menu; Caramelised Pear Bruschetta (page 110)
for dessert completes the Italian scenario. This salad is also perfect with a
barbecued butterflied leg of lamb for a one-course summer supper.

Halve onion then cut each half into thin even-sized wedges

Lift out and discard the hard strip of the centre core from each wedge

Slice zucchini halves on the diagonal into thin wedge-shaped pieces

roasted vegetable and balsamic salad

PREPARATION TIME **10 minutes** ● COOKING TIME **25 minutes**
SERVES 4

$^1/_4$ cup (60ml) olive oil

1 clove garlic, crushed

2 large green zucchini (300g)

4 medium flat mushrooms
   (500g), quartered

4 large egg tomatoes (360g), quartered

1 medium red onion (170g),
   cut into wedges

150g lamb's lettuce, trimmed

$^1/_3$ cup loosely packed,
   coarsely chopped basil

dressing

$^1/_4$ cup (60ml) olive oil

2 tablespoons balsamic vinegar

$^1/_2$ teaspoon sugar

$^1/_2$ teaspoon dijon mustard

1 clove garlic, crushed

1 Preheat oven to hot. Combine oil and garlic in small bowl. Halve zucchini lengthways then chop into thin wedge-shaped pieces on the diagonal.

2 Arrange vegetable pieces, in single layer, on oven trays, brush with garlic-flavoured oil; roast, uncovered, in hot oven about 20 minutes or until browned lightly and just tender. Remove vegetables from oven; cool.

3 Combine cold vegetables in large bowl with lettuce and basil. Add dressing; toss to combine.

dressing Combine ingredients in a glass screw-top jar; shake well.

per serving 28.2g fat; 1321kJ

TIPS

● Combine garlic and oil a day ahead, and cover at room temperature, in order to infuse the oil with the full flavour of the garlic.
● "Flat" mushrooms are sometimes sold as "field" mushrooms in the supermarket, but this is not strictly correct because they are cultivated. True field mushrooms are those found growing wild; local varieties include the Australian cep, or slippery jack, and the saffron milk cap. Flats are, as the name implies, large flat mushrooms having a rich earthy flavour, and are ideal for filling, roasting or barbecuing.
● Lamb's lettuce, also known as mâche, lamb's tongue or corn salad, has clusters of tiny, tender, nutty-tasting leaves; mild and succulent, lamb's lettuce does not overpower any ingredient it accompanies, but instead allows the other flavours to dominate. You can substitute mesclun, baby mixed salad leaves or butter lettuce, if lamb's lettuce is not available.

Wash and thoroughly dry the coriander before removing roots

Finely chop enough cleaned coriander root to make 2 teaspoons

Coarsely chop enough coriander leaves to make a loosely packed quarter cup

kumara, chilli and coriander soup

PREPARATION TIME 10 minutes ● COOKING TIME 20 minutes
SERVES 4

100g fresh coriander, roots attached

1 tablespoon vegetable oil

1 large brown onion (200g), chopped coarsely

2 cloves garlic, crushed

1½ teaspoons sambal oelek

3 medium kumara (1.2kg), chopped coarsely

1 litre (4 cups) water

2 cups (500ml) chicken stock

⅔ cup (160ml) coconut milk

1 Wash coriander under cold running water, removing any dirt clinging to the roots; dry thoroughly. Finely chop enough of the coriander root to make 2 teaspoons (remaining root can be chopped, wrapped in plastic and frozen for future use); coarsely chop enough coriander leaves to make a loosely packed ¼ cup (freeze remainder of the leaves in the same way you do the roots).

2 Heat oil in large saucepan; cook coriander root, onion, garlic and sambal oelek, stirring, until onion softens.

3 Add kumara; cook, stirring, 5 minutes. Add the water and stock; bring to a boil. Reduce heat; simmer, uncovered, about 15 minutes or until kumara softens.

4 Blend or process soup, in batches, until smooth; return soup to same cleaned pan. Simmer, uncovered, over medium heat until thickened slightly; stir in coconut milk. Divide soup among serving bowls; sprinkle with reserved coriander leaves.

per serving 13.8g fat; 1360kJ

TIPS

● This soup can be made a day ahead and refrigerated, covered.

● Be certain to choose coriander with its roots intact; here, as in many Asian dishes, the roots are used as an ingredient. Sprinkle the fresh coriander leaves over each bowl of soup just before serving to wilt but not overcook them.

● Kumara is sometimes called sweet potato at the greengrocer's; its flesh is orange rather than off-white in colour, and its appearance often causes it to be confused for the tuber called yam. Cooked kumara is also delicious mashed with butter or cream and a dash of nutmeg.

SERVING SUGGESTION
Either our Char-Grilled Baby Octopus Salad (page 62)
or Pork and Broccolini Stir-Fry (page 45)
will serve as a complementary main course
to this richly warming, spicy opener.

SERVING SUGGESTION
This simple but utterly delectable pasta starter is
happily followed by the more complex and robust
flavours of our Spicy Sausages with Lentils (page 42)
or Slow-Roasted Portuguese Chicken (page 33).

Roast the pine nuts in a small, heavy-based frying pan to release their fragrance

Remove and discard the longer or thicker stems from the rocket leaves

Make long, thin flakes of parmesan by using a vegetable peeler

spaghetti with rocket, parmesan and pine nuts

PREPARATION TIME 5 minutes ● COOKING TIME 10 minutes

SERVES 4

200g spaghetti
1/4 cup (60ml) olive oil
2 cloves garlic, crushed
1 large red thai chilli, chopped finely
1/4 cup (40g) roasted pine nuts
1/2 cup (40g) flaked parmesan cheese
100g baby rocket leaves

1 Cook pasta in large saucepan of boiling water, uncovered, until just tender.

2 Meanwhile, heat oil in small saucepan; cook garlic and chilli, stirring, about 30 seconds or until garlic just softens and is fragrant (do not brown the garlic).

3 Place drained pasta and oil mixture in large bowl with pine nuts, cheese and rocket; toss to combine.

per serving 24.6g fat; 1700kJ

TIPS

● Roast pine nuts in an ungreased heavy-based frying pan over medium heat, stirring constantly, until pine nuts are golden brown. You'll find it easier to roast small amounts (say, 1/2 cup or less) of tiny nuts or nut pieces (such as pine nuts, almond slivers, etc) this way rather than in the oven. Remove them from the hot pan as soon as they start to become aromatic or they'll continue to cook and probably scorch. Roasting nuts helps release their dormant flavours.

● Lash out and use extra virgin olive oil in this recipe (it's as much of an ingredient as the pasta, garlic and chilli so should be of a high quality). The same goes for the parmesan – buy a piece of the best available and flake it yourself using a vegetable peeler.

● Substitute the rocket leaves with baby spinach leaves if desired. Take the time to trim the tough part of the stems of both rocket and spinach: it's not crucial to the success of the dish but it adds to both its appearance and texture.

● All pastas have varying cooking times, plus each cook has his or her own idea of the right degree of tenderness. Start by following directions on the pasta packet, but test pasta 1 to 2 minutes short of the suggested cooking time. Keep testing until the sample is cooked to your taste. When cooking long strands of pasta, add it to a large saucepan filled with plenty of rapidly boiling water to which you've already added a hefty pinch of salt. To reheat pasta, pour boiling water over it while in a colander placed inside a large saucepan. Gently separate pasta pieces with a fork, then lift colander from pan to drain.

Split each piece of pide horizontally before toasting both sides

Slice bocconcini and tomatoes into similar sized pieces

Shred basil by rolling leaves into cigar shape then slicing across with a sharp knife

bruschetta caprese

PREPARATION TIME **15 minutes**

SERVES 4

*This appetiser is a clever blend of two classic Italian dishes: salad caprese and a typical bruschetta.
While bruschetta is traditionally made using a wood-fired bread such as ciabatta, this break with convention
provides a more stable base for the topping and is easier to cut with a table knife.*

1 long loaf pide

50g baby rocket leaves

250g cherry tomatoes, sliced thickly

**100g baby bocconcini cheese,
   sliced thickly**

2 tablespoons finely shredded fresh basil

2 tablespoons extra virgin olive oil

1 Halve pide; reserve one half for later use. Cut remaining half crossways into four even-width pieces. Split each piece horizontally; toast both sides.

2 Place two slices toasted pide on each of four serving plates. Top each slice with equal amounts of rocket, tomato, cheese and basil, then drizzle with oil.

per serving 15.9g fat; 1691kJ

TIPS

● Use goat cheese for a stronger, tangy flavour instead of bocconcini and, if you want to add more colour to the topping, use equal amounts of red cherry and yellow teardrop tomatoes.

● Long ovals of pide are simply called Turkish bread in some supermarkets; pide is also available in individual rounds.

● A fairly new variety of small tomato is available at most supermarkets and greengrocers. Called "grape tomatoes" because of their shape, they are slightly tangier than cherry tomatoes, and full of flavour.

● Bocconcini is a delicate, semi-soft, white cheese traditionally made in Italy from buffalo milk; it spoils rapidly so can only be kept, refrigerated in brine, for 1 or 2 days at most. "Baby" bocconcini are about the size of a cherry tomato; regular bocconcini, the size of golf balls, can be substituted as can ordinary mozzarella, but both must be sliced to a similar thickness as the sliced tomato.

SERVING SUGGESTION
Either our Shellfish Paella Risotto (page 69) or
Lamb Cutlets with White Bean Salad (page 50) would be perfect
after this Italian first course; end the meal with corella pears
and a piece of gorgonzola, the creamy blue cheese from
the Lombardy region of Italy.

Chop onion extremely finely then reserve a quarter of it for the salsa

Holding the edge of a tortilla with both hands, slide it in and out of the tomato mixture

Place some of the chicken and cheese in a row, close to the edge of each tortilla

chicken enchiladas with corn salsa

PREPARATION TIME 30 minutes ● COOKING TIME 35 minutes

SERVES 4

If you've ever had doubts about cooking Mexican food, you'll soon see that making a meal like this is quite easy and far more delicious than what's on offer in most Latino restaurants.

1 large red onion (300g), chopped finely

2 tablespoons vegetable oil

2 cloves garlic, crushed

1 tablespoon tomato paste

1/4 cup (45g) drained bottled jalapeño chillies, chopped coarsely

400g can tomatoes

1 cup (250ml) chicken stock

500g chicken breast fillets, sliced thinly

10 corn tortillas

2 cups (250g) coarsely grated cheddar cheese

1/2 cup (120g) sour cream

corn salsa

1 small red capsicum (150g), chopped finely

310g can corn kernels, drained

1 tablespoon lime juice

1 cup loosely packed, coarsely chopped fresh coriander

1 Reserve a quarter of the onion for the corn salsa (below). Preheat oven to moderate.

2 Heat oil in large frying pan; cook remaining onion with garlic, stirring, until onion softens. Add tomato paste, chilli, undrained crushed tomatoes, stock and chicken; bring to a boil. Reduce heat; simmer, uncovered, until chicken is cooked through. Remove chicken from pan; cover to keep warm.

3 Soften tortillas in oven or microwave oven, according to manufacturer's instructions. Dip tortillas, one at a time, in tomato mixture in pan; place on board. Divide chicken and half of the cheese among tortillas, placing along edge; roll tortilla to enclose filling. Place enchiladas, seam-side down, in large oiled 3-litre (12-cup) shallow ovenproof dish; enchiladas should fit snugly, without overcrowding.

4 Pour remaining mixture over enchiladas; top with sour cream, sprinkle with remaining cheese. Bake, uncovered, in moderate oven about 15 minutes or until heated through.

5 Divide enchiladas among serving plates; serve with corn salsa.

corn salsa Place reserved onion in small bowl with capsicum, corn, juice and coriander; toss to combine.

per serving 51.6g fat; 3152kJ

SERVING SUGGESTION
Precede the enchiladas with a bowl of warmed corn
chips and quick-as-a-flash homemade guacamole –
accompanied, of course, by a frosted jug of margaritas.

SERVING SUGGESTION
These pies are great accompanied by a mixed green salad
tossed in a classic French vinaigrette made with red wine
vinegar. Lash out on dessert: our Brownie Ice-Cream Stacks
with Hot Fudge Sauce (page 106) is appropriately indulgent!

Clean leek by fanning it apart under cold running water

Discard the stalks of tarragon after gently pulling away individual leaves

Top chicken mixture in baking dishes with pastry rounds brushed with beaten egg

tarragon chicken and leek pies

PREPARATION TIME 15 minutes ● COOKING TIME 45 minutes

SERVES 4

40g butter

660g chicken thigh fillets, chopped coarsely

200g button mushrooms, halved

1 large leek (500g), sliced thickly

1 tablespoon plain flour

1/2 cup (125ml) dry white wine

3/4 cup (180g) sour cream

1 tablespoon dijon mustard

1 tablespoon coarsely chopped fresh tarragon

1 sheet ready-rolled butter puff pastry

1 egg, beaten lightly

1 Preheat oven to moderately hot.

2 Melt half of the butter in large frying pan; cook chicken, in batches, until browned all over.

3 Melt remaining butter in same pan; cook mushrooms and leek, stirring, about 5 minutes or until leek is tender. Stir in flour; cook, stirring, until flour browns slightly. Stir in wine; cook, stirring, until mixture boils and thickens. Stir in chicken, sour cream, mustard and tarragon.

4 Divide filling among four 1 1/2-cup (375ml) ovenproof dishes.

5 Cut four 10cm rounds from pastry. Brush edges with egg; top chicken mixture with pastry. Use a fork or spoon to decorate edges; brush pastry with egg. Make small cuts in pastry to allow steam to escape. Bake pies, uncovered, in moderately hot oven about 20 minutes or until pastry is browned lightly.

per serving 49.3g fat; 2959kJ

TIPS

● Remove any fat from chicken thigh fillets before chopping them. You could substitute chicken breast fillets here but you'll find that the thighs' more distinct flavour suits the mustard and tarragon best.

● To rid leeks of hidden grit, cut the root off leek then slice it lengthways through the white section; next, hold leek by the green half under cold running water and fan the white leaves apart to rinse away any dirt. Cut off the green half and discard before chopping leek in wheels.

● Make sure to use a wine in this recipe that's good enough to drink with the pies; we used a chablis.

● Pull tarragon leaves off the stalks before coarsely chopping them.

Smash olives with the side of a heavy knife to make seeding easier

Crush toasted saffron threads with the back of a small wooden spoon

Finely chopping preserved lemon helps disperse its flavour through the tagine

chicken tagine with olives and preserved lemon

PREPARATION TIME 15 minutes ● COOKING TIME 45 minutes

SERVES 4

In Morocco, the word "tagine" refers both to a slowly cooked stew and the special cone-topped pottery casserole dish in which it is served.

1 tablespoon olive oil

1 tablespoon butter

8 chicken thigh cutlets (1.3kg), skinned

1 large red onion (300g), chopped finely

1/2 teaspoon saffron threads, toasted, crushed

1 teaspoon ground cinnamon

1 teaspoon ground ginger

1 1/2 cups (375ml) chicken stock

16 seeded large green olives (120g)

2 tablespoons finely chopped preserved lemon

1 Heat oil and butter in large heavy-based saucepan with tight-fitting lid; cook chicken, in batches, until browned all over.

2 Place onion and spices in same pan; cook, stirring, until onion softens. Return chicken to pan with stock; bring to a boil. Reduce heat; simmer, covered, about 30 minutes or until chicken is cooked through.

3 Remove chicken from pan; cover to keep warm. Skim and discard fat from top of sauce; bring to a boil. Reduce heat; cook, stirring, until sauce reduces by half.

4 Return chicken to pan with olives and lemon; stir over medium heat until heated through.

per serving 25.9g fat; 1831kJ

TIPS

● Saffron, the stigma of a crocus, is said to be the world's most expensive spice because it is so labour-intensive to harvest and process. The good news, however, is that since only minuscule amounts are called for in recipes, a tiny jar of deep-red-orange saffron threads will last you for ages if carefully kept, tightly sealed, in your freezer.

● Avoid using powdered saffron because it's usually made from the crocus stamen or a blend of turmeric and other dried spices. Saffron threads should be toasted in a small dry frying pan over medium heat until they are just fragrant, then crushed with the back of a spoon or crumbled directly over the saucepan.

● Preserved lemons, an important condiment in North African cooking, can now be found in most large supermarkets. Lemon pieces are packed in a salt mixture and left until the rind becomes soft and pulpy, at which time it is chopped finely and stirred into chicken or meat stews (tagines) to add an intense tartness. Rinse preserved lemon well under cold water before chopping.

SERVING SUGGESTION
Serve steamed jasmine rice with the chicken,
following it with a large bowl of chopped
tropical fruit salad which includes pawpaw,
pineapple, starfruit and mango, all drizzled
with cooled Star-Anise Syrup (page 102).

Trim banana leaf into 30cm squares, discarding the centre rib

Chop lemon grass into tiny pieces, starting from the white end of the stalk

Loosely pack the coarsely chopped coriander into the measuring cup

steamed chicken in banana leaf

PREPARATION TIME **25 minutes** ● COOKING TIME **15 minutes**

SERVES 4

4 single chicken breast fillets (680g)

5 cloves garlic, crushed

1 tablespoon grated fresh ginger

1/4 cup finely chopped fresh lemon grass

2 red thai chillies, chopped finely

1/2 cup loosely packed, coarsely chopped fresh coriander

1/3 cup (80ml) lime juice

1 1/2 tablespoons peanut oil

1 large banana leaf

300g snow peas, trimmed

1/4 cup (40g) roasted pine nuts

dressing

2 tablespoons lime juice

2 tablespoons brown sugar

1 tablespoon rice wine

1 tablespoon fish sauce

1/2 teaspoon sesame oil

1/2 teaspoon grated fresh ginger

1 clove garlic, crushed

2 teaspoons sweet chilli sauce

1 Using sharp knife, make three shallow cuts on smooth side of each fillet.

2 Combine garlic, ginger, lemon grass, chilli, coriander, juice and oil in large bowl. Press spice mixture all over chicken, pressing firmly but gently into cuts. Cover; refrigerate while preparing banana leaf.

3 Cut banana leaf into four 30cm squares. Using tongs, dip one square at a time into large saucepan of boiling water; remove immediately. Rinse under cold water; pat dry with absorbent paper. Leaves should be soft and pliable.

4 Centre each fillet on a banana leaf square. Fold leaf over fillet to enclose; secure each parcel with kitchen string. Place parcels in bamboo steamer over wok or large saucepan of boiling water; steam, covered, about 15 minutes or until chicken is cooked through.

5 Meanwhile, boil, steam or microwave snow peas until just tender. Rinse under cold water; drain. Combine snow peas in medium bowl with pine nuts; add dressing. Toss to combine; serve snow peas with chicken.

dressing Combine ingredients in glass screw-top jar; shake well.

per serving 24.2g fat; 1838kJ

Turn drumsticks with metal tongs so that you don't pierce the skin

Use a vegetable peeler to slice kumara into long, paper-thin strips

Strain the cooled deep-frying oil through a paper-towel-lined sieve before refrigerating

roasted spicy chicken drumsticks with kumara chips

PREPARATION TIME **20 minutes** ● COOKING TIME **40 minutes**

SERVES 4

²/₃ cup (200g) yogurt

2 cloves garlic, crushed

1 tablespoon ground cumin

1 tablespoon ground coriander

2 tablespoons finely chopped fresh mint

12 chicken drumsticks (1.8kg)

2 small kumara (500g)

vegetable oil, for deep-frying

1 Preheat oven to hot.

2 Combine yogurt, garlic, cumin, coriander and mint in large bowl. Add chicken; toss to coat each drumstick all over in yogurt mixture. Place chicken, in single layer, in large shallow oiled baking dish.

3 Roast chicken, uncovered, in hot oven 20 minutes. Using metal tongs, turn chicken; spoon pan liquid over each drumstick then roast, uncovered, further 20 minutes or until chicken is cooked through.

4 Meanwhile, using vegetable peeler, slice peeled kumara into long, thin ribbons. Heat oil in medium frying pan; deep-fry kumara, in batches, until lightly browned. Drain on absorbent paper.

5 Serve chicken with kumara chips.

per serving 43.9g fat; 2907kJ

TIPS

● Chicken wings can be substituted for drumsticks. Buy large wings: 12 of these will weigh about 1.5kg and be enough to serve four people adequately.
● Chicken can be marinated in the yogurt mixture overnight and refrigerated, covered.
● Discard the stalks before chopping mint leaves as these can give a bitter flavour to the marinade.

● Brush the yogurt marinade over the drumsticks occasionally while roasting chicken.
● You can substitute the kumara with other tubers or root vegetables to make chips: try deep-frying thinly sliced parsnips, carrots, turnips or beetroots – mix and match them according to colour!

● Don't waste the oil you've used for deep-frying: it can be cooled then poured into a glass jar with a tight-fitting lid and refrigerated. Apply commonsense when using the same oil for different foods: for instance, strong-tasting fish will leave its mark on the oil and render it unsuitable for other foods. Cooled oil may need to be strained though a muslin- or paper-towel-lined sieve.

SERVING SUGGESTION
Start the meal with our Kumara, Chilli and Coriander Soup (page 12):
the subtle South-East Asian flavours of both recipes are quite
complementary. Serve the drumsticks on top of mounded baby
lettuce leaves, tossed with shredded mint and the juice of a lemon.

SERVING SUGGESTION
For an entree, cook frozen wontons or gow gees according to package instructions; serve, dipped in a mixture of soy sauce and freshly chopped chilli, while you're preparing this simple and quick main course. Chicken skewers and bok choy can be accompanied by steamed jasmine rice.

Crush sichuan peppercorns before combining with the other spices

Sprinkle combined spice mixture onto skewered chicken with your fingers

Wash the leaves of the baby bok choy after you have quartered it lengthways

salt and pepper chicken skewers on baby bok choy

PREPARATION TIME **10 minutes** ● COOKING TIME **15 minutes**
SERVES 4

You need 12 skewers for this recipe; if using bamboo skewers, soak them in water for an hour before using to avoid splintering or scorching.

8 chicken thigh fillets (880g), chopped coarsely

1 teaspoon sichuan peppercorns, crushed

1/2 teaspoon five-spice powder

2 teaspoons sea salt

1 teaspoon sesame oil

600g baby bok choy, quartered

1 tablespoon oyster sauce

1 teaspoon light soy sauce

1 Thread chicken onto 12 skewers. Combine peppercorns, five-spice and salt in small bowl; sprinkle mixture over chicken, pressing in firmly.

2 Cook chicken, in batches, on heated oiled grill plate (or grill or barbecue) until browned all over and cooked through; cover to keep warm.

3 Meanwhile, heat oil in wok or large frying pan; stir-fry bok choy with combined sauces until wilted.

4 Divide bok choy among serving plates; top with chicken skewers. Sprinkle chicken with a little chopped fresh coriander, if desired.

per serving 17.4g fat; 1419kJ

TIPS

● Sichuan (also spelled Szechuan) peppercorns can be crushed in a spice grinder or with a mortar and pestle. A coffee grinder can also be used, if you wipe it out thoroughly both before and after grinding the peppercorns… or you can resort to the old tried-and-true method of smashing them, wrapped in a piece of muslin or sealed in a paper bag, with a meat mallet. Occasionally already crushed sichuan pepper can be found in Asian supermarkets.

● Oyster sauce is an important ingredient in Chinese cooking. It is made from oysters in brine, soy sauce and other seasonings, cooked until so concentrated it is virtually without any seafood taste. Its rich savoury flavour and deep-brown colour enhance food both as an ingredient during cooking and as a condiment for the table. Keep oyster sauce refrigerated after opening.

● Use fingers to press the spice mixture onto the skewered chicken pieces; pat it onto the chicken firmly but gently so that it adheres when the skewers are grilled.

Chicken tenderloins are all meat, with no waste, and can be cooked quickly

Cut baby corncobs in half on the diagonal before cooking them

Snap the asparagus spear's woody base from where it starts to break off naturally

char-grilled five-spice chicken

PREPARATION TIME **15 minutes** ● COOKING TIME **10 minutes**
SERVES 4

750g chicken tenderloins

1 teaspoon peanut oil

1¹/₂ teaspoons five-spice powder

2 cloves garlic, crushed

300g baby corncobs

500g asparagus

1 medium red capsicum (200g),
    sliced thinly

¹/₄ cup loosely packed, coarsely chopped
    fresh flat-leaf parsley

1 Combine chicken, oil, five-spice and garlic in medium bowl.

2 Cook chicken on heated oiled grill plate (or grill or barbecue) until browned and cooked through.

3 Meanwhile, cut baby corncobs in half. Snap woody ends off asparagus; chop remaining spears into same-sized pieces as halved corn. Stir-fry corn, asparagus and capsicum in heated lightly oiled wok or large frying pan until just tender.

4 Stir parsley into vegetables off the heat, then divide mixture among serving bowls; top with sliced chicken.

per serving 16.1g fat; 1646kJ

TIPS

● This is a good recipe to make for a crowd because it's quick and easy to prepare. Increase the amounts above proportionately, according to the number of people you intend to feed. The chicken can be mixed with the oil, spice and garlic the day before required and refrigerated, covered. Prepare the vegetables just before you want to serve this dish.

● Five-spice powder is a fragrant mixture of ground cinnamon, cloves, star anise, sichuan pepper and fennel seeds; you will find it in the Asian section of most supermarkets and in specialist spice shops.
● Baby corncobs are usually sold fresh, packaged by weight, in most greengrocers. In this recipe, you can substitute baby corn with two normal fresh corncobs. Remove husk and silk, then cut each cob into 3cm "wheels" and cook as described above.

● Bend the lower third of each asparagus spear; the end will snap off between the woody base and the flesh of the spear. You may like to peel thicker, tougher spears with a vegetable peeler.
● If you love the taste of fresh coriander, you can substitute it for the coarsely chopped flat-leaf parsley called for in this recipe.

SERVING SUGGESTION

Make this meal heartier by tossing the
cooked vegetables with 500g of heated
hokkien noodles to make a "bed" on
each serving plate for the chicken. For
dessert, make our Banana Soufflés with
Butterscotch Sauce (page 114).

SERVING SUGGESTION
Serve with a mixed green salad and homemade potato wedges, tossed with a blend of olive oil, sea salt, coarsely ground black pepper and sweet paprika before roasting. Make twice as many wedges as you think you'll need because they're very more-ish!

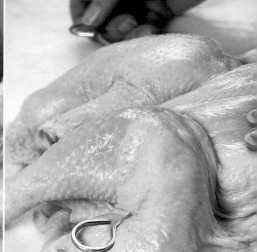

Use kitchen scissors to cut along both sides of the chicken's backbone

Pressing down with the heel of your hand, flatten the breastbone of the chicken

Insert a metal skewer from the thigh through to the opposite wing to keep chicken flat

slow-roasted portuguese chicken

PREPARATION TIME **15 minutes** ● COOKING TIME **2 hours**
SERVES 4

Sometimes known as piri-piri chicken after Portugal's favourite spicy hot sauce, this style of cooking chicken has become a runaway success, winning customers from traditional deep-fried, spit-roast or barbecued chicken shops. With this recipe, you'll find what you make is so delicious you'll never buy takeaway again.

1.6kg chicken

1 red thai chilli, seeded, chopped finely

1 tablespoon sweet paprika

3 cloves garlic, crushed

2 teaspoons salt

1/2 cup (125ml) lemon juice

2 tablespoons olive oil

1 tablespoon coarsely chopped fresh oregano

1 Preheat oven to moderately slow.

2 Wash chicken under cold running water; pat dry with absorbent paper. Using kitchen scissors, cut along both sides of backbone; discard backbone. Place chicken, skin-side up, on board; using heel of hand, press down on breastbone to flatten chicken. Insert metal skewer through thigh and opposite wing of chicken to keep chicken flat. Repeat with other thigh and wing.

3 Combine remaining ingredients in small bowl.

4 Place chicken in large baking dish; pour chilli mixture over chicken. Roast, uncovered, in moderately slow oven, brushing occasionally with pan juices, about 2 hours or until chicken is browned and cooked through.

per serving 39.9g fat; 2170kJ

TIPS

● Add one or two more chillies to the spice mixture if you prefer a hotter flavour – and don't bother seeding them for an even fierier version! The day before you want to cook this recipe, blend chilli, spices, juice and oil in a large baking dish then add chicken. Spoon chilli

marinade all over chicken; cover and refrigerate overnight. Turn the chicken a few times so that the marinade is constantly coating each side.
● Juices remaining in the baking dish after the chicken is cooked can be poured into a small jug and served with the meal.

● You can use chicken pieces rather than a whole chicken if you prefer: try a mixture of whole thighs and drumsticks, marylands or whole breasts... just remember to reduce the cooking time. You can also cook this recipe in a covered or kettle barbecue.

Make sure you cut the chicken breast fillets into similar-sized pieces

Chop coriander leaves coarsely rather than finely for this recipe

Blend cornflour with coconut cream until smooth to avoid it becoming lumpy

coconut chicken masala

PREPARATION TIME **10 minutes** ● COOKING TIME **35 minutes**
SERVES 4

2 tablespoons peanut oil

1 large brown onion (200g), sliced thinly

2 cloves garlic, crushed

1 tablespoon coriander seeds

1 tablespoon ground cumin

1 teaspoon ground turmeric

1 teaspoon ground ginger

1 teaspoon garam masala

1/2 teaspoon ground cardamom

2 teaspoons chilli powder

1 teaspoon coarsely ground black pepper

1.5kg chicken breast fillets, chopped coarsely

1/4 cup (70g) tomato paste

11/2 cups (375ml) chicken stock

1/2 cup (125ml) water

1 teaspoon cornflour

3/4 cup (180ml) coconut cream

2 tablespoons coarsely chopped fresh coriander

1 Heat oil in large saucepan; cook onion and garlic, stirring, until onion softens. Add coriander seeds; cook, stirring, about 1 minute or until seeds start to pop. Add remaining spices; cook, stirring, until mixture is fragrant.

2 Add chicken to pan, turning to coat pieces in spice mixture; cook, stirring, until chicken is just browned.

3 Stir in tomato paste, stock and the water; bring to a boil. Reduce heat; simmer, covered, about 20 minutes or until chicken is cooked through.

4 Blend cornflour with coconut cream in small bowl; stir into chicken curry. Bring to a boil; cook, stirring, until mixture boils and thickens. Just before serving, stir in fresh coriander.

per serving 40.4g fat; 3089kJ

TIP

● Masala, in Indian cooking, is really just the word for spice, and we usually see it coupled with another Hindi word, garam, to mean a blend of ground spices, a blend left up to the individual cook in most Indian homes. Here, you can purchase your garam masala already packaged in most Asian grocery stores (but be warned, the flavour varies immensely depending on the manufacturer).

SERVING SUGGESTION
What's a curry without all the yummy side dishes?
Perfect for this chicken curry are steamed basmati
rice; cucumber and cumin raita; and virtually fat-free
pappadums, puffed in your microwave oven just before
serving time. A platter of pawpaw, mango and pineapple
slices is the perfect end to this typical Indian meal.

SERVING SUGGESTION
Start this meal with a few traditional Middle-Eastern dips such as baba ghanoush or hummus then accompany the quail and pilaf with a large bowl of homemade tabbouleh.

Use kitchen scissors to cut along each side of the quail's backbone

Using fingers of one hand, press the quail, skin-side up, into "butterfly" shape

Break the uncooked vermicelli into uneven lengths but none shorter than 4cm

butterflied marinated quail with pine nut pilaf

PREPARATION TIME 10 minutes ● COOKING TIME 20 minutes
SERVES 4

6 fresh quails (1.2kg)
1/3 cup firmly packed, coarsely chopped
    fresh flat-leaf parsley
3/4 cup (180ml) olive oil
2/3 cup (160ml) lemon juice
3 cloves garlic, crushed
1 tablespoon ghee
75g vermicelli, broken coarsely
1 1/2 cups (330g) basmati rice
2 cups (500ml) chicken stock
1 1/2 cups (375ml) water
1/2 cup (80g) roasted pine nuts

TIPS

● Vermicelli is a very thin spaghetti-like pasta, and using it fried with rice is a traditional Lebanese way of making pilaf, that popular rice dish which is also spelled pilau, pilav or pilao and cooked in a hundred different ways. You can find pre-fried vermicelli sold in Middle Eastern grocery stores.
● Ghee is clarified butter usually found canned in the refrigerated section of the supermarket; substitute equal amounts of butter and olive oil in this recipe if you can't locate the ghee.
● Add a cinnamon stick to the pilaf mixture while it simmers for an aromatic touch; discard cinnamon before serving.

1   Wash quails under cold water; pat dry with absorbent paper. Using kitchen scissors, cut along each side of each quail's backbone; remove and discard backbone. Turn each quail over, skin-side up; use heel of hand to press flat.

2   Reserve about half of the parsley. Combine remaining parsley in large bowl with oil, juice and garlic. Add quails; toss to coat each in parsley marinade. Cover; refrigerate 10 minutes.

3   Heat ghee over medium heat in large saucepan with tight-fitting lid; cook vermicelli and rice, stirring, about 2 minutes or until vermicelli is golden brown and rice almost translucent. Add stock and the water; bring to a boil. Reduce heat; simmer, covered, about 20 minutes or until liquid is absorbed and pilaf is cooked as desired.

4   Meanwhile, cook quails on heated oiled grill plate (or grill or barbecue), brushing occasionally with parsley marinade, until browned both sides and cooked through. Keep four quails whole; cut remaining two quails in half down the middle. Discard any remaining marinade.

5   Just before serving, stir pine nuts and remaining parsley through pilaf. Divide pilaf among serving plates, topping each with 1 1/2 quails.

per serving 79.3g fat; 5071kJ

Push cooked potatoes, in batches, through a sieve with a wooden spoon

Only turn each piece of beef once to avoid it becoming too tough and unyielding

Press beef with fingers to test if it is cooked as desired – never pierce it with a knife

beef fillet with horseradish mash

PREPARATION TIME **10 minutes** ● COOKING TIME **30 minutes**

SERVES 4

**4 medium potatoes (800g),
    chopped coarsely**

1/2 cup (120g) sour cream

1/4 cup (60ml) milk

1 tablespoon horseradish cream

600g beef eye fillet

1 cup (250ml) dry red wine

1/2 cup (125ml) beef stock

1 tablespoon seeded mustard

1 Boil, steam or microwave potatoes until tender; drain. Mash potatoes with sour cream and milk in large bowl until smooth; stir in horseradish cream.

2 Meanwhile, slice beef into four equal pieces. Cook on heated oiled grill plate (or grill or barbecue) until browned both sides and cooked as desired; remove beef from pan. Cover; stand 5 to 10 minutes.

3 Meanwhile, combine wine, stock and mustard in medium saucepan; bring to a boil. Reduce heat; simmer, uncovered, until sauce reduces by half.

4 Serve beef topped with sauce, accompanied by mash and steamed asparagus, if desired.

per serving 20.7g fat; 2041kJ

TIPS

● You can also use either rump or scotch fillet in this recipe. We cooked our beef medium-rare in about 5 minutes; adjust cooking time to suit your taste. Be certain the grill plate is well-heated before the beef touches it; this immediately seals in the juices. To avoid the meat toughening, never turn it more than once during the entire cooking time.

● Don't mash potatoes in a food processor as they break down to a gluey puree. Kitchen tools that can be used to mash potatoes are a potato ricer (good if you are only dealing with a few potatoes) or a mouli (food mill), both of which are available from cookware shops. You can also push hot cooked potatoes through a large sieve using the back of a wooden spoon.

● We used red burgundy in this recipe, but any dry red wine could be used. Just remember that if a wine's not good enough to drink, it's not good enough to use in cooking. Avoid using leftover wine that has been opened for a while. If you prefer not to use alcohol, increase the amount of beef stock by a cup and add a tablespoon of balsamic vinegar.

SERVING SUGGESTION
This classic main course can follow a traditional prawn cocktail
or simple tomato soup starter. In keeping with the traditional
European theme, go for a simple chocolate mousse or
tarte tatin for dessert.

SERVING SUGGESTION
Start with a salad of rocket, sliced tomatoes and bocconcini
dressed in a parsley and lemon vinaigrette, and end the meal with
a simple Italian dessert like zabaglione, that delectable blend
of egg yolks, wine and sugar whisked into a cloud-like foam.

Stir polenta constantly to avoid it becoming lumpy

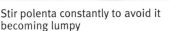

Smooth polenta into oiled pan then pat down so that it's an even depth throughout

Shaking beef with the flour inside a plastic bag guarantees even coating

beef ragù with grilled polenta

PREPARATION TIME 20 minutes (plus refrigerating time) ● COOKING TIME 1 hour 30 minutes
SERVES 4

Ragù, from the French ragoût, is an Italian food term referring to slow-cooked meat-based dishes. A ragù can either be made with mince or a single large chunk of meat; both require the addition of other ingredients, such as bacon, onions or mushrooms, to become complete.

1 litre (4 cups) water

1 teaspoon salt

1 cup (170g) polenta

1/2 cup (40g) finely grated
   parmesan cheese

1 egg yolk

1kg beef chuck steak

plain flour

2 rashers bacon (140g)

200g button mushrooms

1 tablespoon olive oil

20g butter

1 large brown onion (200g),
   chopped coarsely

2 cloves garlic, crushed

1 cup (250ml) dry red wine

1 cup (250ml) beef stock

1/4 cup (70g) tomato paste

1 tablespoon dijon mustard

1 tablespoon finely chopped fresh thyme

1 Place the water and salt in large saucepan; bring to a boil. Add polenta in a slow, steady stream, stirring constantly. Reduce heat; simmer, uncovered, stirring constantly, about 20 minutes or until polenta thickens. Stir in cheese and egg yolk. Spread polenta mixture into oiled deep 19cm-square cake pan; press firmly to ensure even thickness. When cool, cover; refrigerate about 2 hours or until firm.

2 Meanwhile, cut away and discard as much fat as possible from beef; cut into 3cm pieces. Toss beef in flour; shake off excess. Cut off and discard rind from bacon; coarsely chop bacon. Trim mushroom stems; halve mushrooms.

3 Heat oil in large heavy-based saucepan; cook beef, in batches, stirring, until browned all over.

4 Heat butter in same pan; cook onion, garlic, bacon and mushrooms, stirring, until onion softens. Return beef with any juices to pan. Add wine, stock, paste, mustard and thyme; bring to a boil. Reduce heat; simmer, covered, about 1¹/₄ hours or until beef is tender, stirring occasionally.

5 Turn polenta onto board; trim edges. Cut polenta into four squares; cut each square in half diagonally. Cook polenta triangles on heated oiled grill plate (or grill or barbecue) until browned both sides. Serve ragù over polenta triangles.

per serving 29.1g fat; 3127kJ

Pierce each sausage casing a few times to let the excess fat drain out

Turn the cooking sausages with a wooden spoon or tongs to ensure they brown all over

Pick out and discard bay leaves after lentils have softened

spicy sausages with lentils

PREPARATION TIME 5 minutes ● COOKING TIME 35 minutes

SERVES 4

1 tablespoon olive oil

2 teaspoons black mustard seeds

1 large brown onion (200g),
   chopped coarsely

2 cloves garlic, crushed

3 bay leaves

6 large egg tomatoes (540g),
   chopped coarsely

1 cup (200g) red lentils

1¹/₂ cups (375ml) vegetable stock

¹/₂ cup (125ml) dry white wine

¹/₂ cup (125ml) water

8 spicy beef sausages (600g)

1 Heat oil in large heated frying pan; cook seeds, onion, garlic and bay leaves, stirring, until onion softens. Add tomato and lentils; cook, stirring, 2 minutes.

2 Add stock, wine and the water; bring to a boil. Reduce heat; simmer, uncovered, stirring occasionally, 15 minutes. Discard bay leaves before serving.

3 Meanwhile, pierce sausages with fork; cook, uncovered, in separate large heated frying pan, until browned all over. Serve spicy sausages with lentils.

per serving 44.4g fat; 2758kJ

TIPS

● Piercing the sausage cases not only lets some of the fat escape out into the frying pan where you can drain it away, but it also helps prevent the possibility of the sausage splitting, especially if you happen to be cooking sausages over very high heat on a grill plate, barbecue or in a microwave oven.

● We used spicy Italian beef and herb sausages here, but you can experiment among the wide variety of sausages available nearly everywhere, until you find one you particularly like. Other recommended sausages are merguez, spicy lamb adopted by the French from their origin in Morocco, or Italian pork and fennel sausages.

SERVING SUGGESTION
This homely, flavoursome dish is great
balanced with a simple coleslaw tossed
in a caraway-flavoured vinegar dressing.
And don't forget the bread – perfect to
scoop clean the bowl! For dessert, our
Apple and Rhubarb Crumble (page 113)
provides a fitting companion dish.

SERVING SUGGESTION
Start this meal with pan-fried beef or
chicken dumplings (sometimes called
pot-stickers or gyoza), available frozen
at all Asian supermarkets; serve the stir-fry
with steamed white rice and end with fresh
lychees in our Star-Anise Syrup (page 102).

Slice pork steaks thinly into 5mm strips before stir-frying

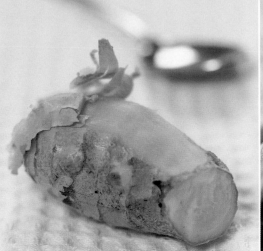

Peel ginger by using the bowl of a small spoon to scrape off the skin

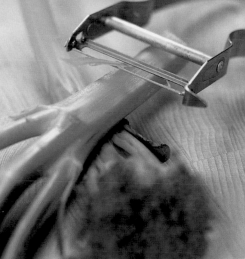

If stems of the broccolini are especially thick or tough, peel before halving the sections

pork and broccolini stir-fry

PREPARATION TIME **15 minutes** ● COOKING TIME **20 minutes**

SERVES 4

2 tablespoons peanut oil

450g pork steaks, sliced thinly

1 medium red onion (170g), sliced thinly

**1 medium red capsicum (200g),
   sliced thinly**

1 clove garlic, crushed

1 teaspoon grated fresh ginger

300g broccolini

1 teaspoon cornflour

2 tablespoons lemon juice

1/4 cup (60ml) water

1/4 cup (60ml) sweet chilli sauce

1 teaspoon fish sauce

1 tablespoon light soy sauce

1 teaspoon sesame oil

**1 tablespoon coarsely chopped
   fresh coriander**

1 tablespoon coarsely chopped fresh mint

1 Heat half of the peanut oil in wok or large frying pan; stir-fry pork, in batches, until browned.

2 Heat remaining peanut oil in wok; stir-fry onion, capsicum, garlic and ginger until vegetables are just tender.

3 Meanwhile, trim and halve broccolini. Blend cornflour with juice in small bowl; add the water, sauces and sesame oil. Stir mixture to combine.

4 Return pork to wok with broccolini and cornflour mixture; stir-fry about 2 minutes or until mixture boils and thickens slightly. Remove from heat; stir in coriander and mint just before serving.

per serving 15g fat; 1234kJ

TIPS

● Ginger can be peeled by using the edge of the bowl of a small spoon to scrape away the skin (you'll find this quicker than trying to navigate a vegetable peeler through the ginger's crevices). Freeze any ginger you have left by breaking the unpeeled knob into smaller pieces, wrapping and freezing them individually.

● Have everything ready for the stir-fry (including the steamed rice) so that it can be eaten as soon as it has finished cooking.
● Heat oil in wok before adding the first batch of pork so that the meat sears immediately instead of stewing and becoming soggy rather than crisp.

● Broccolini, a cross between chinese broccoli and broccoli, actually bears a resemblance to asparagus both in flavour and texture. If you are unable to find broccolini, you can use chinese broccoli or choy sum instead.

Peel whole garlic cloves before slicing them as thinly as possible

Toss couscous with a fork to fluff it as you add herbs so that it doesn't clump

Whisk lemon juice into yogurt and mint to make the sauce smooth and creamy

lime-marinated lamb loin and herbed couscous

PREPARATION TIME **15 minutes** ● COOKING TIME **10 minutes**

SERVES 4

800g lamb eye of loin

2 cloves garlic, sliced thinly

1/4 cup (60ml) lime juice

2 tablespoons olive oil

2 cups (500ml) chicken stock

2 cups (400g) couscous

1/4 cup loosely packed coarsely chopped fresh coriander

yogurt sauce

200g plain yogurt

1/4 cup coarsely chopped fresh mint

2 tablespoons lime juice

1 Combine lamb, garlic, juice and half of the oil in large bowl. Cover; refrigerate 15 minutes.

2 Meanwhile, place stock and remaining oil in medium saucepan; bring to a boil. Remove from heat; add couscous. Cover; stand about 5 minutes or until liquid is absorbed. Using fork, toss coriander into couscous.

3 Cook lamb, in batches, on heated oiled grill plate (or grill or barbecue) until browned all over and cooked as desired. Rest 5 minutes then slice lamb thinly and serve with couscous and yogurt sauce.

yogurt sauce Combine ingredients in small bowl.

per serving 19.2g fat; 3082kJ

TIPS

● Toss chopped flat-leaf parsley or mint leaves through the couscous if you don't care for coriander; a teaspoon or two of finely grated lime rind can also be added to the hot stock just before you stir in the couscous.

● Lamb eye of loin, sometimes sold as backstrap, is extremely tender, with very little wastage. You can substitute an equal weight of lamb fillets if you prefer.

● Any extra lime juice can be frozen in an ice-cube container for future use. Always roll limes on kitchen bench to extract as much juice as possible, and remove the rind before juicing.

SERVING SUGGESTION
This recipe is so simple and at the same
time so elegant that you should choose a
starter and dessert to match. The flavours
of this dish complement our Lime and
Coconut Delicious dessert (page 109).

SERVING SUGGESTION
Make our Roasted Tomato Soup (page 7)
to have as a first course then serve a mixed
green salad dressed in a red wine and garlic
vinaigrette with this main meal.

Soften the onion without browning it before adding sugar and vinegar

Turnips and celeriac make a delicious mash that is as good as (or better than) traditional potato

Mash parsnip and potato together with a hand masher then add sour cream and milk

lamb sausages with caramelised red onion and parsnip mash

PREPARATION TIME **15 minutes** ● COOKING TIME **30 minutes**

SERVES 4

60g butter

1 clove garlic, crushed

4 medium red onions (680g), sliced thinly

2 tablespoons sugar

2 tablespoons red wine vinegar

6 medium parsnips (600g),
   chopped coarsely

2 medium potatoes (400g),
   chopped coarsely

1/2 cup (120g) sour cream

1/4 cup (60ml) milk

8 lamb sausages (800g)

2 tablespoons finely chopped fresh
   flat-leaf parsley

1 Heat butter in large frying pan; cook garlic and onion, stirring, until onion softens and browns lightly. Add sugar and vinegar; cook, stirring, about 15 minutes or until mixture caramelises.

2 Meanwhile, boil, steam or microwave parsnip and potato, separately, until tender; drain. Combine parsnip and potato in large bowl with sour cream and milk; mash until smooth.

3 Cook sausages on heated oiled grill plate (or grill or barbecue) until browned all over and cooked through.

4 Serve sausages and parsnip mash topped with caramelised onion and sprinkled with parsley.

per serving 61.5g fat; 4227kJ

TIPS

● Ordinary white or brown onions work just as well when caramelising. Balsamic, malt or cider vinegar can be used in place of red wine vinegar, and brown sugar can be substituted for ordinary white sugar. If refrigerated, caramelised onion will solidify; reheat it gently to soften the mixture. You can do this, covered, on HIGH for about 30 seconds in a microwave oven.

● There are a few simple rules to follow when making a perfect mash: you should work quickly, never allowing the cooked vegetables to get cold; always heat the ingredients you intend to stir into the mash; and never try to mash potatoes in a food processor because they break down into a gluey puree. Celeriac or turnip can be substituted for the parsnip.

● Kitchen tools (besides a hand-held potato masher) that can be used to mash vegetables, are a potato ricer (good if you are only mashing small amounts) or a mouli (food mill), both of which are available from cookware shops. You can also push the softened hot vegetables through a large sieve, using the back of a wooden spoon.

Rinse beans in a sieve with cold water to wash away the can liquid

Seed cucumbers using a small spoon then finely chop them into small pieces

Seed tomatoes by running a knife through the seed pockets of the flattened wedges

lamb cutlets with white bean salad

PREPARATION TIME **10 minutes** ● COOKING TIME **10 minutes**

SERVES 4

12 lamb cutlets (800g)

**2 x 300g cans white beans,
    rinsed, drained**

**3 large egg tomatoes (270g), seeded,
    chopped finely**

**2 lebanese cucumbers (260g), seeded,
    chopped finely**

1 small red onion (100g), chopped finely

1/4 cup (60ml) lemon juice

1 tablespoon seeded mustard

1/3 cup (80ml) olive oil

**2 tablespoons coarsely chopped fresh
    flat-leaf parsley**

1   Cook cutlets, in batches, on heated oiled grill plate (or grill or barbecue) until browned both sides and cooked as desired.

2   Place remaining ingredients in medium bowl; toss to combine. Serve cutlets with white bean salad.

per serving 53.6g fat; 2439kJ

TIPS

● Many varieties of already softened white beans are available canned, among them cannellini, butter and haricot beans; any of these are suitable for this salad.

● You can use loin chops or chump chops in place of the cutlets; depending on their size, you might reduce the quantities to two per serving, if desired.

● We cooked our lamb to medium-rare; adjust cooking time to suit your taste. To avoid toughening the cutlets, never turn them more than once during cooking.

● Standing the cutlets while you're assembling the bean salad allows the meat to "relax" and the juices to "settle".

● Purple shallots (available seasonally from some greengrocers) or spring onions may be used instead of the red onion.

● Any type of tomato may be used in place of egg tomatoes; cherry or teardrop need only be halved if you want to use these. The larger egg tomatoes should be seeded first because the seeds and juice will dilute the dressing and make the salad too wet.

● If you'd like this salad "hotter", add 1 seeded, finely chopped red thai chilli to the oil before adding it to the salad bowl. It's best not to assemble the salad until you're ready to serve the meal.

SERVING SUGGESTION
Start this meal with our spicy
Kumara, Chilli and Coriander
Soup (page 12), accompanied
by warm cornbread.

SERVING SUGGESTION
Our Roasted Vegetable and Balsamic Salad (page 11) is a great choice as a starter for this recipe; toss the vegetables with mixed baby salad leaves just before serving. For dessert, buy four pieces of baklava from your nearest good deli.

Stud lamb with garlic and oregano by pressing it into cuts in the meat

Make sure you cook flour long enough to brown away any "floury" taste in the gravy

Cut across the grain when slicing the lamb, which should be so tender it almost falls apart

slow-roasted greek lamb

PREPARATION TIME 30 minutes ● COOKING TIME 4 hours 15 minutes
SERVES 4

2kg leg of lamb

3 cloves garlic, quartered

¹/₄ cup loosely packed fresh oregano

¹/₂ cup (125ml) dry white wine

1 cup (250ml) chicken stock

¹/₃ cup (80ml) lemon juice

1kg tiny new potatoes,
    quartered lengthways

2 medium lemons (280g), quartered

²/₃ cup (80g) black olives, seeded

1 tablespoon olive oil

2 tablespoons plain flour

1 cup (250ml) water

1 Preheat oven to hot. Using sharp knife, pierce 12 cuts into lamb; press garlic and oregano into cuts.

2 Place lamb in large flameproof baking dish; pour wine, stock and juice over lamb. Cover tightly; roast lamb in hot oven 30 minutes. Reduce temperature to moderate; roast lamb, covered tightly, brushing occasionally with pan juices, further 3 hours or until lamb is extremely tender.

3 Meanwhile, place potato, lemon and olives in separate large baking dish; drizzle with oil. When lamb has about 1 hour left to roast, place baking dish with potato mixture in oven; roast, uncovered, until browned and tender.

4 Transfer lamb to serving dish; cover to keep warm.

5 Heat 1 tablespoon of the reserved lamb juices in same flameproof baking dish; stir in flour. Cook, stirring, until mixture is well browned. Gradually stir in remaining lamb juices and the water; stir until gravy boils and thickens.

6 Slice lamb; serve with potato mixture and gravy.

per serving 27.8g fat; 3431kJ

TIPS

● Look for a lean leg of lamb; any fat should be a pale cream colour. Keep lamb wrapped loosely in foil, under refrigeration, until you're ready to begin cooking.

● To assist juicing, bring lemons to room temperature then roll each one, pressing down firmly, on kitchen bench. This helps release juice from the pulp; any excess juice can be frozen in an ice-cube container.

● Rest the roast 10 to 15 minutes before slicing so that its juices "settle" the meat. When slicing lamb, cut across the grain. Lamb may be so tender it virtually falls apart as you're slicing it.

When grating orange rind, take care not to include any bitter white pith

Use a vegetable peeler to remove the skin from kumara before chopping it coarsely

Turn pork steaks in the marinade to ensure they are coated all over

pork with orange mustard sauce on kumara mash

PREPARATION TIME **10 minutes** ● COOKING TIME **30 minutes**
SERVES 4

4 medium pork steaks (550g)
1 clove garlic, crushed
1 teaspoon grated fresh ginger
1 tablespoon marmalade
1 teaspoon finely grated orange rind
2 tablespoons orange juice
2 tablespoons olive oil
1kg kumara, chopped coarsely
20g butter
1 tablespoon maple syrup
50g butter, extra
2 tablespoons seeded mustard
1/2 cup (125ml) orange juice, extra
1/2 cup (125ml) dry white wine
1/4 cup (60ml) chicken stock
1/4 cup (60g) sour cream

1 Combine pork in large bowl with garlic, ginger, marmalade, rind, juice and half of the oil.

2 Boil, steam or microwave kumara until tender; drain. Mash kumara in large bowl with butter and maple syrup; cover to keep warm.

3 Meanwhile, drain pork; reserve marinade. Heat remaining oil in large frying pan; cook pork, in batches, until browned both sides and cooked as desired. Cover to keep warm.

4 Heat extra butter in same frying pan; cook mustard, extra juice, wine, stock and reserved marinade. Bring to a boil; reduce heat. Simmer, uncovered, about 5 minutes or until sauce reduces by half. Remove sauce from heat; stir in sour cream. Serve kumara with pork; drizzle with sauce.

per serving 34.8g fat; 2698kJ

TIPS

● Maple syrup is a pure product, distilled from the sap of the maple tree; maple-flavoured syrup (ie, pancake syrup) is not an adequate substitute as it's made from sugar cane. While maple syrup is more expensive than the flavoured version, remember that a bottle or can of it will last a long time and it is far superior in flavour.
● Kumara is sometimes called sweet potato at the greengrocer's; its flesh is orange rather than off-white in colour, and its appearance often causes it to be confused for the tuber called yam. Kumara is also delicious baked in its skin, just like white potato, and dotted with butter to serve.

SERVING SUGGESTION
Our Caramelised Pear Bruschetta
(page 110) is the perfect follow-up
to this pork main course, connected
as they are by the citrus and brown
sugar/maple flavours. Accompany
the pork with steamed snow peas.

SERVING SUGGESTION
Serve either Roasted Tomato Soup (page 7)
or Kumara, Chilli and Coriander Soup (page
12) before this main course, and our White
Chocolate and Honeycomb Mousse (page 105)
will bring the meal to a spectacular finish.

Trim any excess fat from pork before brushing it with marinade

The three salad greens can be rinsed together under cold water then drained in a colander

Wasabi comes as a paste in a tube, as well as a powder in a small can

teriyaki pork with wasabi dressing

PREPARATION TIME **10 minutes** ● COOKING TIME **15 minutes**

SERVES 4

750g pork fillets

1/4 cup (60ml) teriyaki marinade

50g snow pea sprouts

100g mesclun

50g watercress, trimmed

1 medium red capsicum (200g),
**   sliced thinly**

250g yellow teardrop tomatoes, halved

wasabi dressing

1 1/2 teaspoons wasabi powder

1/4 cup (60ml) cider vinegar

1/3 cup (80ml) vegetable oil

1 tablespoon light soy sauce

1 Trim pork; brush with teriyaki marinade. Cook pork, in batches, on heated oiled grill plate (or grill or barbecue), brushing frequently with marinade, until browned both sides and cooked as desired; cover to keep warm.

2 Meanwhile, combine sprouts, mesclun, watercress, capsicum and tomato in large bowl.

3 Pour wasabi dressing over salad mixture; toss gently to combine. Slice pork; serve with salad.

wasabi dressing Blend wasabi powder with vinegar in small jug; whisk in remaining ingredients.

per serving 23g fat; 1799kJ

TIPS

● This recipe would be just as good with fish (such as salmon or tuna steaks) as it is with pork fillets.
● Cherry or grape tomatoes can be used instead of the teardrop.

● Snow pea sprouts, mesclun and watercress can be found at most greengrocer's. The three, when combined, give this recipe a distinctively exciting flavour; however, you can substitute any or all of the three with various other greens (such as thinly sliced snow peas, young radicchio, baby rocket leaves or mustard cress) if you cannot find those suggested.

● Wasabi, fiery hot Japanese horseradish, is also available in tubes already made up into a paste. If you have a tube of wasabi, add 1/4 teaspoon of the paste to the other dressing ingredients, whisk to combine, then taste for flavour. Add more, a 1/4 teaspoon at a time, until you attain the heat you desire.

Carefully tear off the hard beige shell to release the small light green beans

Mash potato and extra cream in a large bowl with a hand masher until the mixture is smooth

Using a wooden spoon, gently marble the broad bean puree through the potato mash

lemon veal steaks with broad bean mash

PREPARATION TIME 20 minutes ● COOKING TIME 20 minutes

SERVES 4

500g frozen broad beans, thawed, peeled

4 medium potatoes (800g),
   chopped coarsely

2 tablespoons cream

40g butter

1/2 cup (125ml) cream, extra

8 veal schnitzels (720g)

1 tablespoon finely shredded lemon rind

1/4 cup (60ml) lemon juice

1 clove garlic, crushed

1 tablespoon drained capers,
   chopped coarsely

2 tablespoons olive oil

2 tablespoons coarsely chopped
   fresh chives

1 Boil, steam or microwave beans and potato, separately, until tender; drain. Blend or process beans with cream until smooth. Mash potato in large bowl with butter and extra cream until smooth. Add bean mixture to potato mash; using a wooden spoon, gently marble beans through potato.

2 Meanwhile, cook veal, in batches, in large heated lightly oiled non-stick frying pan until veal is browned both sides and cooked as desired.

3 Serve veal on broad bean mash; drizzle with combined remaining ingredients.

per serving 40g fat; 2834kJ

TIPS

● Don't mash potatoes in a food processor as they break down to a gluey puree. Kitchen tools that can be used to mash potatoes are a hand-held potato masher as shown above or a mouli (food mill), both of which are available from cookware shops. You can also push hot cooked potatoes through a large sieve using the back of a wooden spoon.

● There are many types of potatoes available, and some are better suited to being mashed than others. Pink fir apple, sebago, desiree, king edward and nicola are a few of the potato varieties that are particularly good mashed; try all of them until you find the one you prefer.

● Broad beans, also known as fava, windsor and horse beans, are available dried, fresh and frozen. Fresh and frozen beans are best peeled twice (discarding both the outer long green pod and the beige tough inner shell).

SERVING SUGGESTION
Serve a caesar salad at the
beginning of this meal then lash
out on an extravagant dessert
like our Banana Soufflés with
Butterscotch Sauce (page 114).

SERVING SUGGESTION
A mini mezze of mixed Middle Eastern appetisers can be
purchased at your local delicatessen the day you serve this
main course – buy hummus, baba ghanoush, mini falafel,
a few different types of olives and fresh pitta ... and you've
got a Lebanese banquet with no fuss at all.

Mix kofta mixture with one hand until it forms a smooth paste

Roll tablespoons of kofta mixture into golf-ball shapes then refrigerate 1/2 hour to firm them up

Use your hand to squeeze out as much water from the soaked burghul as possible

lamb kofta with tabbouleh

PREPARATION TIME 35 minutes ● COOKING TIME 15 minutes
SERVES 4

1kg lamb mince

1 medium brown onion (150g), chopped finely

1 egg white

2 tablespoons finely chopped fresh flat-leaf parsley

2 tablespoons finely chopped fresh mint

1 tablespoon finely grated lemon rind

3 teaspoons ground cumin

2 cloves garlic, crushed

1/4 teaspoon chilli powder

1/2 cup (80g) burghul

2 cups loosely packed, coarsely chopped fresh flat-leaf parsley, extra

1/4 cup loosely packed, coarsely chopped fresh mint, extra

2 medium tomatoes (380g), seeded, chopped finely

1 small red onion (100g), chopped finely

2 green onions, sliced thinly

1 lebanese cucumber (130g), seeded, chopped finely

1/4 cup (60ml) olive oil

1/4 cup (60ml) lemon juice

1 clove garlic, crushed, extra

4 large pitta breads, quartered

minted yogurt

200g yogurt

1 tablespoon coarsely chopped fresh mint

2 tablespoons lemon juice

1 Using your hand, combine mince in large bowl with brown onion, egg white, parsley, mint, rind, cumin, garlic and chilli powder. Roll tablespoons of kofta mixture into balls; place on tray. Cover; refrigerate 30 minutes. (You will have 32 kofta.)

2 Meanwhile, cover burghul with cold water in small bowl; stand 15 minutes. Drain; squeeze burghul with hand to remove as much water as possible.

3 Place burghul in large bowl with extra parsley and extra mint, tomato, red and green onions, cucumber, oil, juice and extra garlic; toss to combine. Cover tabbouleh; refrigerate.

4 Cook kofta, in batches, on heated oiled grill plate (or grill or barbecue) until browned all over and cooked through. Sandwich two kofta in each pitta quarter; spoon in tabbouleh. Drizzle with minted yogurt.

minted yogurt Combine ingredients In small bowl.

per serving 35.5g fat; 3775kJ

Crushing garlic with the flat side of a knife causes the skin to fall away

Peel ginger by scraping away the skin using the bowl of a small spoon

Use the same spoon to carefully scrape away cucumber seeds

char-grilled baby octopus salad

PREPARATION TIME 20 minutes (plus marinating time) ● COOKING TIME 10 minutes
SERVES 4

750g cleaned baby octopus

1 clove garlic, crushed

1 teaspoon grated fresh ginger

2 teaspoons dry sherry

1 teaspoon brown sugar

1 teaspoon malt vinegar

1/2 teaspoon sesame oil

2 teaspoons kecap manis

2 teaspoons sweet chilli sauce

1/4 cup (60ml) tomato sauce

250g cherry tomatoes, halved

1 small red onion (100g),
   sliced thinly

150g mesclun

2 lebanese cucumbers (260g),
   seeded, sliced thinly

1/3 cup firmly packed,
   coarsely chopped fresh coriander

dressing

1/4 cup (60ml) sweet chilli sauce

1 tablespoon light soy sauce

1 clove garlic, crushed

1 tablespoon lime juice

1 Combine octopus in large bowl with garlic, ginger, sherry, sugar, vinegar, oil, kecap manis and sauces; toss to coat octopus in marinade. Cover; refrigerate 3 hours or overnight.

2 Just before cooking octopus, combine tomato, onion, mesclun, cucumber and coriander in large bowl.

3 Char-grill (or barbecue or pan-fry) undrained octopus, in batches, until browned all over and cooked as desired. Combine octopus with salad in bowl. Add dressing; toss gently to combine.

dressing Combine ingredients in glass screw-top jar; shake well.

per serving 3.3g fat; 923kJ

TIPS

● If you are unable to find cleaned baby octopus, buy 1kg of whole baby octopus; remove and discard heads and beaks from all then cut each octopus in half.
● Marinating the octopus tenderises it, so the longer it "soaks", the better... and the taste of the spices will be more dominant too. We recommend you marinate the octopus a day ahead and refrigerate it, covered tightly.
● Char-grilling octopus outdoors on your barbecue gives it a good crisp finish, but cooking it indoors on a grill plate until brown and crisp on the outside but tender and soft within, the way it's prepared in many Chinese restaurants, is equally successful.
● Ginger used in a marinade doesn't have to be peeled if it is young (without many knobs, fairly smooth-skinned). However, it's easy to peel a small amount by using the edge of the bowl of a small spoon (or a small vegetable knife) to scrape away the skin (you'll find this quicker than trying to navigate a vegetable peeler through the ginger's crevices).

SERVING SUGGESTION
This main course salad is perfect for a Sunday
barbecue: serve fresh oysters chilled, on
the half shell, with fresh lime wedges, while
you're grilling the octopus.

SERVING SUGGESTION
Prepare your favourite fresh Asian noodle –
hokkien, stir-fry or rice – then, after draining,
twirl them on each serving plate to make a
bed for the scallops and salsa; serve with
plenty of lemon wedges and a separate bowl
of sweet chilli sauce.

Sprinkle salt mixture onto scallops so each one is coated evenly

After removing the outermost layer, slice green onions into thin pieces on the diagonal

Roll room-temperature lemon on bench to extract as much juice as possible

salt and pepper scallops with cherry tomato salsa

PREPARATION TIME 20 minutes ● COOKING TIME 10 minutes

SERVES 4

1kg scallops

2 teaspoons sea salt

1/2 teaspoon cracked black pepper

2 cloves garlic, crushed

1 tablespoon peanut oil

cherry tomato salsa

400g cherry tomatoes, quartered

2 lebanese cucumbers (260g), seeded, chopped finely

1 medium red onion (170g), chopped finely

4 green onions, sliced thinly

2 tablespoons lemon juice

2 red thai chillies, seeded, chopped finely

1 Combine scallops with salt, pepper and garlic in medium bowl; use fingers to sprinkle salt mixture evenly over each scallop. Cover; refrigerate 15 minutes.

2 Heat oil in wok or large frying pan; stir-fry scallops, in batches, until salt-pepper coating is browned and scallops are cooked as desired.

3 Add scallops to cherry tomato salsa; toss gently to combine.

cherry tomato salsa Combine ingredients in large bowl.

per serving 6.6g fat; 912kJ

TIPS

● Fresh scallops have a sweet scent and a moist shimmer to the meat; they should also be an off-white, even slight pink, in colour (those that are completely white have probably been soaked in water to make them heavier). Refrigerate scallops as soon as you can after purchasing them, and use them within 2 days. Whether you use the coral-coloured roe that is attached is up to you: we chose to discard it in this recipe.

● To get the perfect colour on the stir-fried scallops (or on any food you want to remain crisp after stir-frying), it's important that the wok or frying pan is heated first, so it is extremely hot when you add the oil. This helps give the food the right crispness, seals in its juices and keeps it from stewing and turning an unfortunate grey in colour.

● This is also why scallops are stir-fried "in batches", so that the wok remains hot throughout the cooking period, searing the scallops all over. Cooking "in batches" means that the just-browned scallops are removed from the wok before the next batch of uncooked scallops is added; this prevents overcrowding and stewing rather than crisping.

Use your fingers to devein prawns after shells have been removed

Cover noodles with boiling water in a heatproof bowl then separate with a fork

Cut each of the baby bok choy into quarters lengthways then rinse under cold water

hokkien noodles with prawns

PREPARATION TIME **20 minutes** ● COOKING TIME **10 minutes**

SERVES 4

24 large uncooked prawns (1.2kg)

500g hokkien noodles

300g baby bok choy

2 teaspoons peanut oil

1 red thai chilli, chopped finely

1 clove garlic, crushed

¹/₄ cup (60ml) water

2 tablespoons sesame oil

¹/₂ cup (125ml) kecap manis

¹/₄ cup (60ml) light soy sauce

¹/₂ cup loosely packed, coarsely chopped fresh coriander

1   Shell and devein prawns, leaving tails intact.

2   Place noodles in large heatproof bowl; cover with boiling water. Use fork to separate noodles; drain. Rinse again by pouring boiling water over noodles in colander; drain. Cut bok choy into quarters lengthways.

3   Heat half of the peanut oil in wok or large frying pan; stir-fry chilli and garlic briefly, until just fragrant. Add prawns, in batches; stir-fry over high heat until just changed in colour.

4   Heat remaining peanut oil in wok; stir-fry noodles and bok choy over high heat until bok choy just wilts.

5   Return prawns to wok with the water, sesame oil, kecap manis, sauce and coriander; stir-fry briefly over high heat until prawn mixture is just hot.

per serving 12.9g fat; 1716kJ

TIPS

● You can use any fresh Asian noodle you like in this recipe – hokkien, stir-fry or rice – but check the manufacturer's instructions regarding the required length of time they are to be soaked (or cooked) in hot water before using because they all differ.

● It is important that the wok or frying pan you use is heated first so that it is extremely hot when you add the oil. This seals in the prawns' juices, preventing them from becoming tough.

● Stir-frying in batches keeps the wok as hot as possible so prawns change to a coral-pink in colour without overcooking. Likewise, when you return prawns to the wok at the end of cooking time, only stir-fry the mixture long enough to reheat the prawns, not overcook them.

SERVING SUGGESTION
Make peking duck rolls to serve before this stir-fry. Buy a
barbecued duck and a packet of pekingese pancakes at an
Asian food store, then remove and shred duck meat before
wrapping portions of it, with a trimmed green onion, in a
warmed pancake spread with a little hoisin sauce.

SERVING SUGGESTION
Serve an antipasti platter, as a starter, consisting of black
and green olives, fetta, anchovies, fried sardines, salami
and pickled artichoke hearts – your choices will only be
limited by your imagination.

Remove fibrous beards from mussels by scrubbing then pulling away firmly

Seed unpeeled tomato pieces by scraping away the juicy seed sections with a small sharp knife

Flake cooked salmon with a fork before stirring it into the risotto

shellfish paella risotto

PREPARATION TIME 30 minutes ● COOKING TIME 45 minutes
SERVES 4

The distinctive flavours of a Spanish paella combine with the soft and creamy texture of an Italian risotto to make this unique – and divine – rice dish.

24 medium uncooked prawns (600g)

16 large black mussels (500g)

200g salmon fillet

3 cups (750ml) chicken stock

3 cups (750ml) water

1/2 cup (125ml) dry white wine

4 saffron threads, toasted, crushed

1 large red capsicum (350g)

2 large tomatoes (500g)

1 cup (125g) frozen peas

1 tablespoon olive oil

1 large brown onion (200g),
    chopped finely

2 cloves garlic, crushed

1½ cups (300g) arborio rice

1 Shell and devein prawns, leaving tails intact. Scrub mussels; remove beards. Heat small lightly oiled frying pan; cook salmon until browned both sides and just cooked through.

2 Combine stock, the water, wine and saffron in large saucepan; bring to a boil. Reduce heat; simmer, covered, over low heat.

3 Meanwhile, cut capsicum in half lengthways. Discard seeds and membranes; chop capsicum finely. Peel tomatoes; seed and chop finely. Rinse peas under hot water; drain.

4 Heat oil in large saucepan; cook onion, garlic and capsicum, stirring, until onion softens. Add rice; stir to coat in onion mixture. Stir in 1-cup batches of the hot stock mixture; cook, stirring, until liquid is absorbed after each addition. Total cooking time should be about 35 minutes or until rice is just tender and all the liquid has been absorbed.

5 Add prawns and mussels; cook, stirring, until prawns change in colour and mussels open. Discard any mussels that do not open. Add tomato, peas and flaked salmon; stir gently until risotto is heated through.

per serving 10.5g fat; 2260kJ

TIPS

● Saffron threads should be toasted in a small dry frying pan over medium heat until they are just fragrant, then crushed with the back of a spoon (or crumbled with your fingers directly over the saucepan).

● Arborio rice is a short, fat white rice capable of absorbing several times its weight in liquid, which is why it's perfect for risotto. It is found in all supermarkets with the other rice varieties.

● Keep the stock mixture, covered, on a low simmer as you're cooking the risotto; frequent additions of cold liquid take the cooking time back to the beginning and tend to startle the rice into being chewy and lacking in firmness.

Cut onion into paper-thin slices then separate them into rings

Stir eggs until the water starts to boil to help centre the yolks

Smashing the olive with the side of a heavy knife makes seeding easy

niçoise salad

PREPARATION TIME **10 minutes**

SERVES 4

The original "salade niçoise", from the French Mediterranean city of Nice, was made of the best of that region's produce: ripe vine tomatoes, local capers, hand-picked baby beans, tiny dark brown olives, anchovies and tuna fresh from the sea, and plump cloves of garlic. No wonder it so delighted foreign visitors to Nice that they took the memory of that salad to all corners of the globe, adapting it slightly, as we have here, to suit their own produce and lifestyle.

3 x 125g cans tuna slices in springwater, drained

1 medium red onion (170g), sliced thinly

250g baby spinach leaves, trimmed

300g can white beans, rinsed, drained

150g yellow teardrop tomatoes, halved

1/2 cup (80g) kalamata olives, seeded

4 hard-boiled eggs, quartered

dressing

1/2 cup (125ml) extra virgin olive oil

1/4 cup (60ml) lemon juice

1 clove garlic, crushed

1 teaspoon coarsely chopped fresh lemon thyme

2 teaspoons dijon mustard

1/4 teaspoon sugar

1 Combine tuna, onion, spinach, beans, tomato, olives and egg in large bowl.

2 Just before serving, pour dressing over salad mixture; toss gently to combine.

dressing Combine ingredients in a glass screw-top jar; shake well.

per serving 36.8g fat; 2038kJ

TIPS

● If you gently stir the eggs until they begin to boil, you will have nicely centred yolks, a good look when they're to be served quartered, as they are here.

● Also consider any of the following to use in this salad: artichoke hearts in oil, sliced radishes, diced cooked potato and roasted green or red capsicum. You can substitute rocket leaves or mesclun for the baby spinach.

● Kalamata olives are small brine-cured black olives; seed them by smashing them with the flat side of a heavy knife then pulling away the seed from the olive flesh. The traditional olive for this salad is the Niçoise, a very small, brownish-black, pointy-ended olive grown in Provence, the French region which skirts the Mediterranean near Monaco. They are delicious but also hard to find and expensive; the kalamata olive is absolutely fine in this recipe.

● If you want to make this dish really special, substitute the canned tuna with about 450g of fresh tuna steaks, brushed with lemon and oil then pan-fried or grilled and cut into bite-sized pieces.

SERVING SUGGESTION
A meal in itself, our salad just needs
to be accompanied by a bottle of dry
white wine and a fresh French baguette
or two. For dessert, we recommend our
Apple and Rhubarb Crumble (page 113).

SERVING SUGGESTION
Serve our Roasted Tomato Soup (page 7)
with these salmon patties and four large
rosetta rolls for a totally scrumptious meal.

Shape mixture into eight patties of the same size and thickness

Coat patties, one after the other, in flour, beaten egg then evenly in breadcrumbs

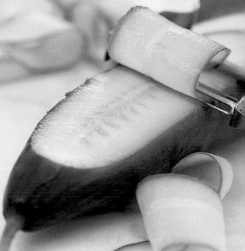

Slice cucumbers lengthways into long, paper-thin ribbons with a vegetable peeler

salmon patties with cucumber and rocket salad

PREPARATION TIME 20 minutes • COOKING TIME 25 minutes

SERVES 4

4 medium potatoes (800g), chopped coarsely

415g can red salmon, drained

4 green onions, chopped coarsely

1/4 teaspoon finely grated lime rind

1/2 cup (75g) plain flour

2 eggs, beaten lightly

1 cup (100g) packaged breadcrumbs

vegetable oil, for shallow-frying

3 lebanese cucumbers (390g)

100g baby rocket leaves

2 red thai chillies, seeded, chopped finely

2 tablespoons lime juice

1 Boil, steam or microwave potatoes until tender; drain. Mash potatoes until smooth; cool 5 minutes. Add salmon, onion and rind; stir until well combined.

2 Using hands, shape salmon mixture evenly into eight patties. Coat each patty with flour, shaking off excess; dip patties in egg then coat evenly with breadcrumbs.

3 Heat oil in large frying pan; cook patties, in batches, until browned both sides.

4 Using a vegetable peeler, slice cucumbers, lengthways, as thinly as possible. Place cucumber ribbons in large bowl with rocket, chilli and juice; toss gently to combine. Serve with salmon patties.

per serving 41.2g fat; 3049kJ

TIPS

● Never try to mash potatoes in a food processor; they break down and become a gluey puree. Kitchen tools that can be used to mash potatoes are a potato ricer (good if you are only mashing a very few potatoes) or a mouli (food mill), both of which are available from cookware shops. You can also push soft hot potatoes through a large sieve using the back of a wooden spoon.

● Different potato varieties absorb different amounts of water when they're cooked, and the method of cooking (steaming, microwaving or boiling) also determines how much water is taken into the cooking potato. Therefore, you may have to experiment to find which potato cooked by what method suits you best; we used pontiac potatoes, boiled then drained in a colander, for these patties.

● Some types of potatoes are better suited to being mashed than others. Pink fir apple, sebago, pontiac, king edward and nicola are a few of the potato varieties that are particularly good mashed; try each of them until you find the one you prefer.

Shave baby fennel as thinly as possible after trimming it

It's far easier to remove or grate the rind of any citrus fruit before you juice it

Cut smoked salmon against the grain into small, even pieces

salmon and fennel spaghetti

PREPARATION TIME **10 minutes** ● COOKING TIME **15 minutes**

SERVES 4

375g spaghetti

1 tablespoon olive oil

4 baby fennel (300g), sliced thinly

2 tablespoons (30g) drained capers

1/2 cup (125ml) dry white wine

1 teaspoon finely grated lime rind

1 tablespoon lime juice

250g smoked salmon

200g crème fraîche

250g baby spinach leaves

1/4 cup finely chopped fresh chives

1 Cook pasta in large saucepan of boiling water, uncovered, until just tender; drain.

2 Meanwhile, heat oil in medium frying pan; cook fennel and capers, uncovered, until fennel softens. Add wine, rind and juice; bring to a boil. Reduce heat; simmer, uncovered, about 5 minutes or until liquid reduces by half.

3 Slice salmon, against the grain, into small pieces; combine with hot pasta and fennel mixture in large bowl. Gently stir in crème fraîche and spinach; sprinkle with chives.

per serving 28.6g fat; 2782kJ

TIPS

● You will be able to prepare the salmon and fennel sauce while the pasta is cooking. Drain pasta then toss with sauce immediately so the hot pasta just wilts the spinach and gently warms the other ingredients.

● Remove stems from baby spinach leaves – not just for appearance but because they add an unpleasant degree of chewiness to this otherwise lusciously smooth dish.

● You can cook pasta earlier in the day; toss a few drops of olive oil through it to keep the strands from sticking together. Just before serving, reheat by pouring boiling water over spaghetti in colander over large saucepan; separate strands with a fork, then lift colander from pan to drain.

● The cooking time for pasta can vary between manufacturers, and cooks have their own ideas about the right degree of tenderness. For dried spaghetti, follow the directions on the packet, but test a strand of pasta 1 to 2 minutes short of the suggested cooking time.

● Substitute crème fraîche with light sour cream if you desire.

SERVING SUGGESTION
The delicacy of this spaghetti is a good foil
for a substantial starter or dessert (or both!):
consider our Roasted Vegetable and Balsamic
Salad (page 11) and Brownie Ice-Cream Stacks
with Hot Fudge Sauce (page 106).

SERVING SUGGESTION
Steamed jasmine rice is all you need to
serve with this fish and stir-fried vegetable
meal; treat your guests to a lavish dessert
to finish off with... our White Chocolate and
Honeycomb Mousse (page 105) fits the bill.

Chop lemon grass as finely as you can, starting from the white end

Top four pieces of fish, skin-side down, with lime leaves and lemon grass

Cover with remaining fish pieces, skin-side up, then tie with kitchen string

slow-roasted ocean trout and asian greens

PREPARATION TIME **15 minutes** ● COOKING TIME **20 minutes**

SERVES 4

8 x 100g ocean trout fillets

2 kaffir lime leaves, shredded finely

2 tablespoons finely chopped fresh lemon grass

1 teaspoon sesame oil

250g baby bok choy, quartered

250g choy sum, chopped coarsely

2 teaspoons light soy sauce

1/3 cup (80ml) sweet chilli sauce

1/4 cup (60ml) lime juice

1 Preheat oven to slow.

2 Place four fish fillets, skin-side down, on board; sprinkle with lime leaves and lemon grass. Top with remaining fish fillets, skin-side up; tie with kitchen string.

3 Place fish in large shallow baking dish; roast, uncovered, in slow oven 15 minutes.

4 Just before serving, heat oil in wok or large frying pan; stir-fry bok choy, choy sum and soy sauce until vegetables just wilt.

5 Serve fish with stir-fried vegetables; drizzle with combined chilli sauce and juice.

per serving 9.7g fat; 1158kJ

TIPS

● It's not without good reason that stir-frying has been the main way of cooking vegetables in Asia for thousands of years: preparation and cooking times are minimal but retention of nutrients and development of flavours are maximised. Almost every vegetable you can think of can be stir-fried successfully, and you'll be pleased to discover that, if you use a well-seasoned wok, you can cook them this way with very little added oil. Make sure vegetables are as dry as possible before stir-frying to prevent them becoming soggy.

● When you use fresh lemon grass, chop it starting from the white end, just up into the green upper part of the stalk (as if you were cutting a green onion). Discard the tough top green section; cut the white part as finely as possible because lemon grass is so tough it never breaks down in cooking.

● Asian sauces help prevent vegetables sticking to the pan – as well as imparting different flavours to the finished dish. Here, we used light soy sauce but you can substitute oyster or mushroom sauce.

● Baby bok choy is sometimes called shanghai bok choy, chinese chard, chinese white cabbage, or baby pak choi; its mildly acrid, distinctively appealing taste has brought baby bok choy to the forefront of commonly used Asian greens. Fast-fried with ginger and garlic, it makes the ideal accompaniment to Peking-style or barbecued duck.

● Choy sum is easy to identify, with its long stems and yellow flowers (hence its other name, flowering cabbage). It is eaten, stems and all, and is good steamed as well as with stir-fries.

Remove any bone fragments from the fish cutlets with tweezers

Blend butter, pesto, pepper and rind in a small bowl until ingredients are well combined

Coat all sides of the fish with the melted butter mixture

blue-eye cutlets with pesto butter

PREPARATION TIME **10 minutes** ● COOKING TIME **10 minutes**

SERVES 4

80g butter

2 tablespoons basil pesto

1/4 teaspoon cracked black pepper

1 teaspoon finely grated lemon rind

4 x 200g blue-eye cutlets

100g baby spinach leaves, trimmed

1 Blend or process butter, pesto, pepper and rind in small bowl until well combined.

2 Cook fish, in batches, in large heated lightly oiled non-stick frying pan until browned both sides and cooked as desired.

3 Place butter mixture in same pan; stir over low heat until butter melts. Return fish to pan; coat with melted butter mixture.

4 Serve fish with baby spinach leaves.

per serving 24.5g fat; 1584kJ

TIPS

● There are many versions of basil pesto that you can buy – some are sold fresh, under refrigeration, while others are available bottled on supermarket shelves. Experiment until you find one you like best. If basil is in season, you can make enough pesto for this recipe quite easily. Just process 1/4 cup fresh basil leaves with 1 clove peeled garlic, 1 tablespoon pine nuts, 2 tablespoons olive oil and 1 teaspoon grated parmesan.

● We used fresh blue-eye cutlets but you can use any firm white fish you prefer – bream, sea perch, swordfish, tuna or whiting; if you don't want to contend with the bone in a cutlet, you can also use boneless, skinless fish in this recipe. Cooking times will change slightly for each different kind and thickness of fish you select; no matter what fish you choose, turn it only once during cooking.

● Check over the fish and remove any bones or skin. Salting your fingers will help give you a better grip when pulling away the skin, and you can use tweezers to pick out any bones.
● Substitute spinach with baby rocket leaves or mesclun if you prefer.

SERVING SUGGESTION
Perfect with an assortment of steamed
baby vegetables such as chats (small
young potatoes), cauliflower and green
beans. Our Apple and Rhubarb Crumble
(page 113) partners this simple main
course quite comfortably.

SERVING SUGGESTION
Make an Indian "tartare sauce" by combining finely chopped lebanese cucumber, chilli, cumin and yogurt. Serve sauce, stir-fried almonds and snake beans, to round out this Indian take on fish and chips deliciously.

After scrubbing kipflers well, cut them lengthways into quarters

Carefully coat kipfler wedges with fragrant hot spice mixture

Shake fish fillets, one at a time, in a plastic bag with flour and curry powder

curried flathead with kipfler wedges

PREPARATION TIME 10 minutes ● COOKING TIME 30 minutes
SERVES 4

750g kipfler potatoes
¹/₃ cup (80ml) peanut oil
2 teaspoons coriander seeds
1 teaspoon garam masala
1 teaspoon sweet paprika
1 teaspoon cardamom seeds
1 teaspoon ground cumin
¹/₄ cup (35g) plain flour
1 tablespoon curry powder
8 medium flathead fillets (800g)
30g butter

1 Preheat oven to moderately hot. Scrub potatoes well then cut lengthways into quarters.

2 Heat oil in medium frying pan; stir coriander, garam masala, paprika, cardamom and cumin over medium heat until seeds pop and spices are fragrant. Add potato; toss to coat pieces all over in spice mixture.

3 Place potato, in single layer, on baking-paper lined oven trays; roast, uncovered, in moderately hot oven about 25 minutes or until browned and crisp.

4 Meanwhile, combine flour and curry powder in plastic bag. Add fish fillets, one at a time; shake bag over bench, holding tightly closed, to coat fish in seasoned flour.

5 Heat butter in large non-stick frying pan; cook fish, in batches, until browned both sides and cooked as desired. Divide fish and wedges among serving plates.

per serving 27.2g fat; 2380kJ

TIPS

● Cook fish on one side then the other, only turning fish once. You'll know when the fish is cooked about halfway through by looking at the side of the fillet – the second side will not take as long to cook as the first.

● Fish is cooked when it is easily flaked in the thickest part. Overcooked fish is tough and dry so follow the theory of "less is more" when frying these fillets.

● We used fresh flathead fillets here, but you can use any firm white fish such as blue-eye, bream, sea perch, swordfish, tuna or whiting.

Stir polenta continuously to ensure it doesn't become lumpy

Pour thickened polenta into the prepared pan with a wooden spoon

Press polenta into an even layer, pushing into corners of the pan with a spatula

grilled herbed polenta with chilli mayonnaise-dressed semi-dried tomato salad

PREPARATION TIME 30 minutes (plus standing time) ● COOKING TIME 25 minutes

SERVES 4

2 cups (500ml) water

2 cups (500ml) vegetable stock

1 cup (170g) polenta

1/2 cup (40g) finely grated
   parmesan cheese

1 tablespoon finely chopped fresh
   flat-leaf parsley

1 tablespoon finely chopped fresh basil

1 red thai chilli, seeded, chopped finely

semi-dried tomato salad

100g mesclun

200g semi-dried tomatoes

4 green onions, sliced thinly

1/4 cup (50g) black olives, seeded,
   sliced thinly

chilli mayonnaise

1 cup (300g) mayonnaise

2 red thai chillies, chopped finely

1/4 teaspoon ground cumin

1/4 teaspoon ground coriander

1/4 teaspoon ground turmeric

pinch chilli powder

1 teaspoon sugar

1 tablespoon lemon juice

1 tablespoon finely chopped fresh
   flat-leaf parsley

1 Place the water and stock in large saucepan; bring to a boil. Add polenta in a slow, steady stream, stirring constantly. Reduce heat; simmer, uncovered, stirring constantly, about 20 minutes or until polenta thickens. Stir in cheese, herbs and chilli.

2 Spread polenta mixture into oiled deep 19cm-square cake pan; press firmly to ensure even thickness. When cool, cover; refrigerate about 2 hours or until firm.

3 Turn polenta onto board; trim edges. Cut polenta into four squares; cut each square in half diagonally. Cook polenta triangles on heated oiled grill plate (or grill or barbecue) until browned both sides.

4 Top polenta with semi-dried tomato salad and chilli mayonnaise.

   semi-dried tomato salad Gently toss ingredients in medium bowl.

   chilli mayonnaise Combine ingredients in small bowl.

   per serving 32.8g fat; 2615kJ

SERVING SUGGESTION

This recipe contains all the elements of food we choose to eat today – fresh, flavoursome and easy to make – so it follows that any other dishes served with it should be of a similar nature. Try our Fruit Salad with Star-Anise Syrup (page 102).

SERVING SUGGESTION
This is quite a rich pasta main meal so it's
best preceded by a light salad or selection
of antipasti and followed by the fresh, clean
flavours of sliced seasonal fruit.

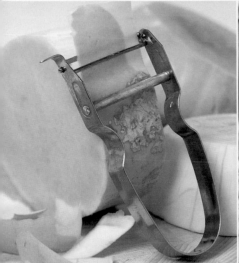

Cut pumpkin into thick slices to make it easier to peel

Toast pepitas and pine nuts in a small heavy-based frying pan, stirring until fragrant

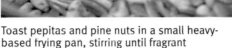

Separate cooked agnolotti by pouring boiling water over them in the colander

spinach and ricotta agnolotti with pumpkin pepita sauce

PREPARATION TIME 10 minutes ● COOKING TIME 50 minutes

SERVES 4

1kg pumpkin

1 tablespoon vegetable oil

625g fresh spinach and ricotta agnolotti

1/4 cup (40g) toasted pepitas

1/2 cup (80g) toasted pine nuts

3/4 cup loosely packed fresh
   flat-leaf parsley

1 small red thai chilli, seeded,
   chopped coarsely

1 clove garlic, quartered

300ml cream

1/4 cup (60ml) peanut oil

1 medium brown onion (150g),
   chopped coarsely

1 Preheat oven to hot.

2 Cut peeled pumpkin into 2cm cubes; place, in single layer, in large shallow baking dish. Drizzle with vegetable oil; roast pumpkin, uncovered, in hot oven about 35 minutes or until tender. Remove from oven; cover to keep warm.

3 Meanwhile, cook pasta in large saucepan of boiling water, uncovered, until just tender; drain.

4 Blend or process pepitas, pine nuts, parsley, chilli, garlic, cream and 2 tablespoons of the peanut oil with half of the pumpkin until mixture is pureed.

5 Heat remaining peanut oil in large frying pan; cook onion, stirring, until soft. Add pasta and pepita mixture; stir over low heat until hot. Serve topped with remaining pumpkin.

per serving 65.2g fat; 4479kJ

TIPS

● Agnolotti is fresh, small, crescent-shaped stuffed pasta, similar to ravioli, available from the refrigerated sections of delicatessens and most supermarkets. If the agnolotti sticks together in the colander after cooking, place the colander over a large saucepan and pour boiling water over the pasta into the pan. Allow to drain a minute or two then separate the pasta gently with a fork and add to the frying pan. You can also use ravioli instead of agnolotti.

● Pepitas are the hulled kernels of pumpkin seeds; olive green in colour, they are usually available roasted, salted or unsalted. They are a common ingredient in Mexican cooking and impart a rich nutty flavour to soups and salsas.

Salt the sliced eggplant then allow it to drain in a colander

Measure the required tomato paste from a tube then seal and refrigerate it for future use

Use a pasta fork to carefully separate the cooked bucatini strands

eggplant and artichoke pasta

PREPARATION TIME 10 minutes (plus standing time) ● COOKING TIME 35 minutes

SERVES 4

1 medium eggplant (300g)

1 tablespoon cooking salt

200g bucatini

1/4 cup (60ml) olive oil

1 tablespoon olive oil, extra

1 medium brown onion (150g),
   sliced thinly

2 cloves garlic, crushed

3 medium tomatoes (570g),
   chopped coarsely

100g button mushrooms, halved

1 small red capsicum (150g), sliced thinly

2 tablespoons tomato paste

400g can artichoke hearts,
   drained, quartered

1 cup (125g) frozen peas, thawed, drained

1 tablespoon coarsely chopped
   fresh basil

1 tablespoon coarsely chopped
   fresh oregano

2/3 cup (50g) finely grated
   parmesan cheese

1 Cut unpeeled eggplant into 1cm slices; place in colander. Sprinkle all over with salt; stand 30 minutes.

2 Meanwhile, cook pasta, uncovered, in large saucepan of boiling water until just tender; drain.

3 Rinse eggplant well under cold running water; pat dry with absorbent paper. Heat oil in large frying pan; cook eggplant, in batches, until browned both sides. Drain eggplant on absorbent paper. Discard any remaining oil in pan; wipe pan clean with absorbent paper.

4 Heat extra oil in same cleaned pan; cook onion and garlic, stirring, until onion softens. Add tomato, mushrooms, capsicum and tomato paste; cook, stirring, until vegetables are just tender.

5 Add artichoke, peas and herbs; cook, stirring occasionally, until mixture is heated through. Add pasta and eggplant; toss gently until hot. Serve immediately, sprinkled with cheese.

per serving 23.8g fat; 1998kJ

TIPS

● Place a weight over eggplant when draining to extract as much of its juice as possible: if left, this liquid causes the slices to soften unattractively or fall apart when cooked. This process is called disgorging, and also helps keep eggplant from absorbing too much oil when cooked.
● Put more, rather than less, salt on the eggplant: it helps draw out the juices and stops the vegetables discolouring. As long as you rinse the drained eggplant well in cold water, you don't run the risk of oversalting the finished dish.

SERVING SUGGESTION
The fresh, salad-like qualities of our
Bruschetta Caprese (page 16) anticipate
the flavours of this hearty main dish.
Continue the Italian theme by making,
earlier in the day, an espresso and
mascarpone-based tiramisu for dessert.

SERVING SUGGESTION
Our Roasted Tomato Soup (page 7) and
Brownie Ice-Cream Stacks with Hot Fudge
Sauce (page 106) make a magnificent
vegetarian feast with this main meal.

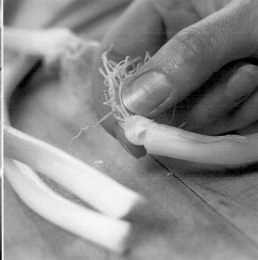

Cook risoni in a large saucepan to avoid overcrowding the pieces

Snap off root end of green onions with fingernail then pull back and remove the outermost layer

Slice zucchini and mushrooms into similar-sized pieces

risoni with mushrooms, zucchini and green onions

PREPARATION TIME 10 minutes ● COOKING TIME 10 minutes

SERVES 4

500g risoni

1 tablespoon olive oil

60g butter

500g zucchini, sliced thinly

300g button mushrooms, sliced thinly

2 cloves garlic, crushed

1 tablespoon coarsely chopped fresh oregano

1 tablespoon lemon juice

1 tablespoon red wine vinegar

200g green onions, sliced thinly

1/2 cup (40g) coarsely grated parmesan cheese

1 Cook pasta in large saucepan of boiling water, uncovered, until just tender.

2 Meanwhile, heat oil with half of the butter in large frying pan; cook zucchini, stirring, until tender and browned lightly. Add remaining butter with mushrooms, garlic and oregano; cook, stirring, 2 minutes then stir in juice and vinegar. Remove from heat; stir in onion and cheese.

3 Place zucchini mixture in large serving bowl with drained pasta; toss gently to combine.

per serving 22.2g fat; 2758kJ

TIPS

● Risoni, like orzo or puntalette, is small rice-shaped pasta. It is great added to soups or baked as a casserole, and as good as rice when served as a main course side dish.

● Slice zucchini and mushrooms into similar-sized pieces so that the finished dish looks balanced and attractive. Cook both of them over high heat; otherwise, both will stew and become soggy and lifeless.

● An average green onion weighs approximately 10 grams so you'll need about 20 of them for this recipe. Buy a large bunch of fresh green onions and chop off and discard most of the green top. Snap off the root end with your fingernail, then pull back and remove the attached skin-like layer. Wrap onions in a paper towel then place the bundle in an airtight plastic bag until ready to use.

Instead of rinsing mushrooms, wipe them over with damp absorbent paper

Trim stems from mushrooms before cutting them in half

Stir rice into the pan in which the mushrooms were cooked

mixed mushroom risotto

PREPARATION TIME **10 minutes** ● COOKING TIME **45 minutes**

SERVES 4

3 cups (750ml) chicken stock

2 cups (500ml) water

1 tablespoon olive oil

200g swiss brown mushrooms, quartered

150g oyster mushrooms, halved

200g button mushrooms, halved

2 cloves garlic, crushed

1 medium brown onion (150g), chopped coarsely

2 cups (400g) arborio rice

1 tablespoon finely chopped fresh tarragon

1/3 cup (80g) sour cream

1 tablespoon seeded mustard

1 Bring stock and the water to a boil in large saucepan. Reduce heat; simmer, uncovered, while cooking mushrooms.

2 Heat half of the oil in large saucepan; cook mushrooms, in batches, until just tender.

3 Heat remaining oil in same pan; cook garlic and onion, stirring, until onion softens. Add rice to pan; stir over medium heat until slightly changed in colour. Stir in 1-cup batches of the hot stock mixture; cook, over medium heat, stirring, until liquid is absorbed after each addition.

4 Add mushrooms and tarragon to risotto when last cup of stock mixture has been added and is almost absorbed. Total cooking time for rice should be about 35 minutes or until rice is just tender. Serve risotto topped with combined sour cream and mustard.

per serving 14.3g fat; 2234kJ

TIPS

● Making a risotto is easy enough, if just a bit time-consuming. The variety of risottos you can make is only limited by your imagination – and what's on hand in your pantry!

● You can use butter rather than olive oil, or equal amounts of each.

● Keep the stock mixture simmering, covered, in another saucepan when you're cooking the risotto: frequent additions of cold liquid take the cooking time back to the beginning and tend to startle the rice into being chewy and too soft.

● If arborio rice is unavailable, use the shortest, most round-grain rice you can find. Long-grain rice will always remain as individual grains, never absorbing enough liquid to achieve the proper soupy-soft texture of a perfect risotto.

SERVING SUGGESTION
All a risotto like this needs to
accompany it is a loaf of warmed
fresh ciabatta or a baguette, and a
bowl of balsamic-dressed rocket with
parmesan flakes.

SERVING SUGGESTION
Serve with a cucumber and cumin raita,
and a small accompanying bowl of
sliced banana and freshly grated
coconut drizzled with lemon juice.

Sort through peas and lentils while rinsing to locate and discard debris

If you don't own a ginger grater, use the smallest holes on one side of a 4-sided grater

Measure the quarter cup of fresh coriander as loosely or firmly packed as you prefer

mixed dhal

PREPARATION TIME **20 minutes** ● COOKING TIME **1 hour 15 minutes**

SERVES 4

1/2 cup (100g) yellow split peas

1/2 cup (100g) brown lentils

2/3 cup (130g) red lentils

20g butter

2 large brown onions (400g),
  chopped finely

3 cloves garlic, crushed

2 teaspoons grated fresh ginger

1 tablespoon black mustard seeds

1 tablespoon ground cumin

1 tablespoon ground coriander

1 teaspoon ground turmeric

1/4 teaspoon chilli powder

2 x 415g cans tomatoes

1 tablespoon tomato paste

11/2 cups (375ml) vegetable stock

1 cup (250ml) water

1/3 cup (80ml) coconut milk

1/4 cup loosely packed,
  coarsely chopped
  fresh coriander

1 Rinse split peas and lentils under cold running water; drain.

2 Melt butter in large saucepan; cook onion, garlic and ginger, stirring, until soft. Add seeds and spices; cook, stirring, about 1 minute or until seeds start to pop.

3 Add split peas, lentils, undrained crushed tomatoes, tomato paste, stock and the water to pan; bring to a boil. Reduce heat; simmer, covered, stirring occasionally, about 1 hour or until split peas and lentils are tender.

4 Add coconut milk; stir over low heat until dhal is heated through. Remove from heat; stir in coriander before serving.

per serving 11.6g fat; 1680kJ

TIPS

● Check over lentils and split peas to ensure they are free of grit or small pebbles.

● If you have access to a shop selling Indian foods, buy masoor dhal (red lentils), moong dhal (brown lentils) and channa dhal (yellow split peas). It's not a bad idea to buy the spices for this recipe at the same place to ensure you're buying them as fresh as possible (turmeric in particular is quite distasteful when stale).

● As soon as the mustard seeds start to pop, add tomatoes and other ingredients – you don't want the seeds and spices to scorch.

● Pack chopped coriander in a quarter-cup measure firmly or loosely, according to your liking of this aromatic herb.

vegetarian 93

Cut pumpkin and zucchini into similar-sized pieces

Line base and side of oiled cake pan with a wide strip of baking paper

Break eggs individually into a small bowl or cup before combining in a medium bowl

zucchini and pumpkin frittata

PREPARATION TIME **15 minutes** ● COOKING TIME **1 hour 10 minutes**

SERVES 4

500g butternut pumpkin, peeled, chopped coarsely

2 large zucchini (300g), chopped coarsely

1 tablespoon olive oil

200g fetta, crumbled

8 eggs

¹/₂ cup (125ml) cream

1 Preheat oven to moderately hot. Oil and line base and side of deep 22cm-round cake pan with baking paper.

2 Combine pumpkin and zucchini, in single layer, in large baking dish; drizzle with oil. Roast, uncovered, in moderately hot oven, about 30 minutes or until vegetables are tender and brown.

3 Reduce oven temperature to moderately slow.

4 Place pumpkin, zucchini and fetta in prepared pan. Break eggs, one at a time, in small bowl then combine in medium bowl; whisk eggs until frothy. Whisk in cream; pour over vegetables and fetta. Bake, uncovered, in moderately slow oven, about 40 minutes or until frittata sets and is just cooked through.

per serving 41g fat; 2101kJ

TIPS

● A frittata is the Italian version of an omelette. Cooked slowly in the oven or on top of the stove over low heat on both sides, a frittata is often cut into squares and eaten in the hands like a sandwich. Fabulous eaten cold or hot, it is different from a traditional omelette because it is cooked through, firm and served open-faced while an omelette is usually soft-centred, moist and folded in half.

● If stove-top cooking a frittata, rather than risk disaster by trying to turn it, once the eggs are just cooked through and almost set, some cooks prefer to place the frying pan briefly under a hot grill to lightly brown the top. You can brown the top of your oven-cooked frittata this way as well, but you must be using a flameproof baking dish or pan to do so.

● We prefer to oven-cook a frittata because it doesn't require the same attention as one cooked on top of the stove. This way, too, pan size and surface material are less important, however, the baking dish or pan used should be made of a material that transmits heat evenly.

SERVING SUGGESTION
Serve with a rocket and pine nut salad,
drizzled with a balsamic dressing, and
warmed rosettas or other fresh bread rolls.

SERVING SUGGESTION

Serve with a bowl of cumin-scented yogurt and warm fresh pitta.

Grate lemon on the finest holes of a 4-sided grater, avoiding the pith

Squeeze 2 tablespoons of juice from the lemon after it's been grated

Toss couscous gently with a fork to ensure the individual grains don't stick together

vegetable couscous

PREPARATION TIME 20 minutes ● COOKING TIME 25 minutes

SERVES 4

350g kumara

1 tablespoon olive oil

60g butter

4 baby eggplants (240g), sliced thinly

1 large brown onion (200g), sliced thinly

1/4 teaspoon cayenne pepper

2 teaspoons ground cumin

2 teaspoons ground coriander

11/2 cups (375ml) vegetable stock

2 cups (400g) couscous

2 teaspoons finely grated lemon rind

2 cups (500ml) boiling water

410g can chickpeas, rinsed, drained

2 tablespoons lemon juice

100g baby spinach leaves

1/4 cup loosely packed fresh
    flat-leaf parsley

1 Chop peeled kumara into 1cm cubes. Heat oil and half of the butter in large frying pan; cook kumara with eggplant and onion, stirring, until vegetables brown. Add spices; cook about 2 minutes or until just fragrant. Stir in stock; bring to a boil. Reduce heat; simmer, uncovered, about 15 minutes or until vegetables are just tender.

2 Meanwhile, combine couscous in large heatproof bowl with half of the remaining butter, rind and the water. Cover; stand about 5 minutes or until water is absorbed, occasionally fluffing couscous with fork.

3 Add chickpeas and remaining butter to vegetable mixture; cook, stirring, until butter melts. Stir in couscous, juice, spinach and parsley.

per serving 20.1g fat; 3246kJ

TIPS

● Kumara is sometimes called sweet potato; its flesh is orange rather than off-white in colour, and its appearance often causes it to be confused with the tuber called yam. Peeled and cooked kumara is also delicious mashed with butter or cream and a dash of nutmeg.

● Grate the lemon using a 4-sided grater, taking care not to incorporate any of the bitter white pith with the rind. Only juice the lemon after it's been grated.

● Couscous, tiny balls of semolina originally from North Africa, has become increasingly popular and is now found in supermarkets everywhere. One reason for this popularity (besides its delicious and adaptable taste) is the speed with which it can be prepared – it can be on the table in far less time than either traditional pasta or rice.

● Remove vegetable mixture from heat, then immediately add couscous, spinach and parsley; the greens will wilt in the heat of the vegetables.

Halve onion and use a knife to remove and discard the hard centre shoot

Using a sharp knife, cut each onion half into six equal-sized wedges

Thread vegetables onto skewers in alternate order

mushroom, tomato and zucchini skewers with white bean puree

PREPARATION TIME **15 minutes** ● COOKING TIME **15 minutes**

SERVES 4

1 large red onion (300g)

200g button mushrooms

250g cherry tomatoes

2 large zucchini (300g), chopped coarsely

2 tablespoons balsamic vinegar

2 tablespoons olive oil

white bean puree

2 x 400g cans white beans, rinsed, drained

1 cup (250ml) chicken stock

1 clove garlic, quartered

1 tablespoon lemon juice

1 tablespoon olive oil

1 Cut onion through the middle into 12 wedges.

2 Thread onion, mushrooms, tomatoes and zucchini equally among 12 skewers. Place skewers on large tray; drizzle with combined vinegar and oil.

3 Cook skewers on heated oiled grill plate (or grill or barbecue) until browned all over and tender.

4 Serve skewers on white bean puree.

white bean puree Combine beans and stock in large saucepan; bring to a boil. Reduce heat; simmer, uncovered, about 10 minutes or until liquid is absorbed. Blend or process bean mixture with garlic, juice and oil until smooth.

per serving 14.7g fat; 882kJ

TIPS

● If you are using bamboo skewers, don't forget to soak them in water at least an hour before threading them with the vegetables; this helps prevent them from scorching or splintering. If you are using metal skewers, wipe them over with olive oil before threading the vegetables to help prevent the vegetables from sticking.

● Many varieties of already cooked white beans are available canned, among them cannellini, butter and haricot beans; any of these are suitable for this puree.
● Substitute drained canned chickpeas for the white beans and a tablespoon of tahini (sesame paste) for the olive oil for a hummus-like puree.

● You can mix and match various baby vegetables in this recipe: tiny patty-pan squash, finger eggplant, golden shallots… even baby cauliflower can all be successfully grilled.
● Trim or halve the vegetables into cocktail-skewer sized portions and serve the mini skewers with drinks at a barbecue.

SERVING SUGGESTION
This vegetarian main dish is wonderful served with
spanakopita (Greek spinach and fetta turnovers),
which can be purchased frozen or already prepared
from delicatessens. For a delicious meat variety,
however, you can serve with grilled lamb cutlets.

SERVING SUGGESTION

This is the perfect meal for a hot summer's night. Thai-style sticky black rice made with coconut milk and served with fresh mango slices makes a delicious dessert.

Place cabbage wedge on its side then use a sharp knife to "shred" it

Rice stick noodles will soften when soaked for a few minutes in a large bowl of hot water

Remove and discard the capsicum seeds and then all of the membrane

rice noodle salad

PREPARATION TIME **20 minutes**

SERVES 4

150g rice stick noodles

1/4 cup (60ml) lime juice

1/4 cup (60ml) sweet chilli sauce

1 tablespoon light soy sauce

1 tablespoon sugar

6 cups (480g) finely shredded red cabbage

1 large carrot (180g), sliced thinly

1 lebanese cucumber (130g), seeded, sliced thinly

3 medium egg tomatoes (225g), seeded, sliced thinly

1 medium yellow capsicum (200g), sliced thinly

1/2 cup firmly packed fresh coriander leaves

1/2 cup firmly packed fresh mint leaves

1/2 cup firmly packed fresh thai basil leaves

1 Place noodles in large heatproof bowl; cover with boiling water. Stand until just tender; drain.

2 Meanwhile, combine juice, sauces and sugar in small bowl; stir until sugar dissolves.

3 Place noodles in large bowl with juice mixture and remaining ingredients; toss to combine thoroughly.

per serving 1.6g fat; 903kJ

TIPS

● You will need about half a medium red cabbage for this recipe. Don't shred the cabbage until you're ready to use it to help preserve its vitamin content. When cutting cabbage into manageable-sized pieces, leaving the core in each wedge will help keep the leaves together. To shred cabbage finely, place a wedge on its side on cutting board; using a large, very sharp knife, slice through the wedge vertically. You can shred it on the single-blade side of a 4-sided grater or in a food processor, using the grating disk.

● Rice stick noodles and dried rice noodles are virtually the same thing, however rice stick noodles are thicker. The two can easily be interchanged in recipes. They do not need cooking but will soften if soaked for about 4 minutes, covered with boiling water, in a large bowl. Pat dry with absorbent paper after soaking so that the dressing isn't diluted.

● Make a non-vegetarian version of this salad by adding 16 medium cooked prawns to the mixture when you add the fresh herbs.

Before halving strawberries, hull them with the tip of a small knife

Use a cherry pitter, if you own one, to make removing the seeds a quick and easy process

Press down on cardamom pods with the side of a heavy knife to bruise them into opening

fruit salad with star-anise syrup

PREPARATION TIME 30 minutes (plus cooling time) ● COOKING TIME 5 minutes
SERVES 4

1 small honeydew melon (900g)

250g strawberries

400g cherries

4 cardamom pods

4 star anise

1/2 cup (110g) caster sugar

1/4 cup (60ml) lemon juice

1/4 cup (60ml) water

1 Halve, peel and chop melon coarsely. Hull strawberries; cut in half. Seed cherries; place fruit in large bowl.

2 Bruise cardamom pods; place in small saucepan with star anise, sugar, juice and the water. Stir over heat, without boiling, until sugar dissolves.

3 Pour warm syrup over fruit; refrigerate, covered, about 30 minutes or until cold.

per serving 0.7g fat; 901kJ

TIPS

● You can make the syrup up to 2 days ahead and refrigerate, covered, until ready to use. Reheat it before pouring over the fruit, as described in step 3 above.

● You can use this syrup with any fruit. For instance, a selection of tropical varieties such as carambola, rambutan, pineapple, mango or mangosteen go well with the anise/cardamom flavour of the syrup.

● Halve and hollow out a second small honeydew melon (blend the flesh with yogurt for a smoothie) and keep the four halves to use as serving "dishes"; sprinkle finely shredded fresh mint over the fruit just before serving.

SERVING SUGGESTION
Dollop with mascarpone and serve after a
Sunday barbecue, or make this recipe the
grand finale of a multi-course Asian banquet.

SERVING SUGGESTION

A rich mousse like this makes a generous finale to a light meal such as our Spaghetti with Rocket, Parmesan and Pine Nuts (page 15). It can also take pride of place in a more extravagant meal for a special occasion.

You can use plain honeycomb rather than the chocolate-covered variety

It's important to beat the egg whites only until they are glossy and barely holding a shape

Using a rubber spatula, gently fold egg whites into white chocolate mixture

white chocolate and honeycomb mousse

PREPARATION TIME **10 minutes (plus cooling time)** ● COOKING TIME **5 minutes**

SERVES 4

2 eggs, separated

250g white chocolate, chopped coarsely

1 tablespoon caster sugar

1 teaspoon gelatine

1/3 cup (80ml) milk

300ml thickened cream

2 x 50g chocolate-coated honeycomb bars, chopped coarsely

1 Place egg yolks, white chocolate, sugar, gelatine and milk in small heavy-based saucepan; stir continuously, over low heat until mixture is smooth. Transfer mixture to large bowl; cool.

2 Beat egg whites, in small bowl, with electric mixer until soft peaks form.

3 Beat cream, in separate small bowl, with electric mixer until soft peaks form.

4 Fold cream and honeycomb into chocolate mixture then fold in egg whites. Divide mixture among four 1-cup (250ml) glasses; refrigerate mousse, covered, for 4 hours before serving.

per serving 55.8g fat; 3209kJ

TIPS

● In this recipe we used Violet Crumble bars, chocolate-dipped honeycomb (a confection made of sugar, glucose and bicarbonate of soda); you can substitute plain honeycomb for the chocolate-covered variety, if preferred. Use the best quality white chocolate you can find.

● Care must be taken when heating the white chocolate mixture: if the heat is too high, the chocolate will "seize", ie, become clumpy, grainy and, therefore, unusable.

● It's a good idea to break eggs, one at a time, into a small cup or jug, or onto a saucer, before adding to a mixture or other eggs. This way, if one egg is stale, you can discard it before adding it to the dish you're preparing. Never use an egg that has been cracked for some time.

Use baking paper to line the base and sides of an 8cm x 26cm bar cake pan

Remove baking paper from the cooled brownie then trim narrow ends before slicing

Cut brownie into 12 even slices before removing ice-cream from the freezer

brownie ice-cream stacks with hot fudge sauce

PREPARATION TIME **20 minutes (plus freezing time)** ● COOKING TIME **45 minutes**

SERVES 4

500ml vanilla ice-cream, softened

80g butter

150g dark chocolate, chopped coarsely

3/4 cup (150g) firmly packed brown sugar

2 eggs, beaten lightly

1/2 cup (75g) plain flour

1/4 cup (60g) sour cream

1/2 cup (50g) coarsely chopped walnuts

hot fudge sauce

50g dark chocolate, chopped coarsely

1/2 cup (125ml) cream

2 tablespoons brown sugar

1/2 teaspoon instant coffee powder

1 tablespoon Tia Maria or Kahlua

1 Line base and sides of 8cm x 26cm bar cake pan with baking paper. Press ice-cream into pan, cover with foil; freeze overnight.

2 Preheat oven to moderate. Line base and sides of another 8cm x 26cm bar cake pan with baking paper.

3 Combine butter and chocolate in small saucepan; stir over low heat until mixture is smooth. Transfer chocolate mixture to medium bowl. Stir in sugar; cool.

4 Stir in eggs then flour, sour cream and nuts. Spread mixture into prepared pan; bake, uncovered, in moderate oven about 40 minutes. Cool brownie in pan.

5 Turn onto wire rack; remove paper. Trim narrow ends; cut brownie into 12 slices.

6 Turn ice-cream out of pan; cut into eight slices. Stack, starting and finishing with brownie, alternate slices of ice-cream and brownie. Drizzle each stack with hot fudge sauce.

hot fudge sauce Combine chocolate, cream, sugar and coffee in small saucepan. Stir over low heat until mixture is smooth; bring to a boil. Reduce heat; simmer, uncovered, 2 minutes. Remove from heat; stir in liqueur.

per serving 68.3g fat; 4471kJ

TIP

● An American classic, the brownie is thought to have been "invented" by accident when a New England housewife inadvertently forgot to add the baking powder to a chocolate cake she was making. Chocolate lovers around the world have enjoyed that result, in one form or another, for more than a century.

SERVING SUGGESTION
Perfect on its own with cups of espresso
after a night out, this brownie recipe is
also good served as a dessert after a
simple meal of soup and salad.

SERVING SUGGESTION
Serve immediately from the oven,
with scoops of vanilla ice-cream melting over
the top, at the conclusion of a roast dinner.

An egg can be separated by carefully using your hand to palm the yolk

Beat egg yolks and sugar in a small deep bowl until mixture is thick and creamy

Grate limes, using the smallest holes on a 4-sided grater, before you juice them

lime and coconut delicious

PREPARATION TIME 8 minutes ● COOKING TIME 50 minutes

SERVES 4

3 eggs, separated

1/2 cup (110g) caster sugar

30g butter, melted

2 teaspoons finely grated lime rind

1/3 cup (80ml) lime juice

1 cup (250ml) milk

1/2 cup (75g) self-raising flour

1/3 cup (30g) desiccated coconut

1/2 cup (110g) caster sugar, extra

1 Preheat oven to moderate.

2 Beat egg yolks and sugar in small bowl with electric mixer until thick and creamy. Transfer to large bowl; stir in butter, rind and juice then milk, flour and coconut.

3 Beat egg whites in small bowl with electric mixer until soft peaks form; with motor operating, gradually add extra sugar, beating until sugar dissolves between additions. Fold egg white mixture, in 2 batches, into lime mixture.

4 Pour into lightly greased deep 1.5-litre (6-cup) ovenproof dish; place in baking dish. Pour enough boiling water into baking dish to come halfway up side of pudding mixture dish.

5 Bake, uncovered, in moderate oven about 50 minutes or until pudding is just set.

per serving 17.7g fat; 1997kJ

TIPS

● It's a good idea to break eggs, one at a time, into a small cup or jug before adding to a mixture or to other eggs. This way, if one egg is stale, you can discard it before adding it to the dish you're preparing. Never use an egg that has been cracked for some time.

● Egg whites should be at room temperature before being beaten, and both the beaters and bowl must be scrupulously clean and dry. Any trace of grease prevents the egg whites from rising to the required volume. For the same reason, when separating eggs, make sure no yolk is included with the whites.

● Remove the rind before you juice the limes. Bring the limes to room temperature then roll, pressing down on lime firmly, on the kitchen bench. This helps release juice from within the pulp. Any extra lime juice can be frozen in an ice-cube tray for future use.

Fold ricotta, ginger and icing sugar lightly into the whipped cream

Cut each of the brioche into four equal slices before toasting them on a grill plate

Cut pears into wedges then, using a small knife, remove and discard the core section

caramelised pear bruschetta

PREPARATION TIME **10 minutes** ● COOKING TIME **10 minutes**
SERVES 4

¹/₃ cup (80ml) thickened cream

1 cup (200g) ricotta cheese

¹/₄ cup (50g) finely chopped crystallised ginger

1 tablespoon icing sugar mixture

6 corella pears (900g)

60g butter

¹/₃ cup (75g) firmly packed brown sugar

¹/₄ cup (60ml) orange juice

2 small brioche (200g)

1 Beat cream in small bowl with electric mixer until soft peaks form; fold in ricotta, ginger and icing sugar.

2 Cut each pear into eight wedges; remove and discard core and peel. Melt half of the butter in large frying pan; cook pear, stirring occasionally, until pear is browned lightly. Add remaining butter and brown sugar; cook, stirring, until pear just starts to caramelise. Add juice; cook, stirring, 1 minute.

3 Meanwhile, cut each brioche into four equal slices; toast until browned lightly both sides.

4 Divide brioche slices among serving plates; top with ricotta mixture then caramelised pear.

per serving 31.5g fat; 2690kJ

TIPS

● Bruschetta is traditionally made by rubbing slices of toasted Italian bread with garlic then drizzling them with extra virgin olive oil, while brioche is a French sweet yeast and egg bread eaten, warm, on its own. We've married the two cultures in this delicious dessert. You can substitute the brioche with challah, the usually plaited yeast-leavened egg bread, traditionally eaten on the Jewish Sabbath.

● When beating cream, the colder the bowl and beaters, the better. Use a small deep bowl for the cream, and beat rapidly.
● Icing sugar mixture contains cornflour to keep it soft and free from lumps; it is the one most used in cooking. The only time pure icing sugar must be used is when decorating cakes. Icing sugar is also called confectioner's or powdered sugar in various parts of the world.

● Choose pears that are slightly underripe for this recipe so they hold their shape when being caramelised. We used the small corella pear but you can use whatever variety you prefer, provided the pears weigh about 900g in total and are quite firm.

This is a wonderful sweet to serve when friends
drop by for tea on a cold winter's afternoon,
yet it is splendid enough to hold its own after a
celebratory company dinner.

SERVING SUGGESTION
Talk about sweet old-fashioned favourites
– this has to be on everyone's list!
Serve as the dessert for a meal having our
Prawn Cocktail with Lime Aioli (page 8)
as the starter and Beef Fillet with Horseradish
Mash (page 38) for the main course.

Peel and core apples before cutting them into thick wedges

After discarding the leaves, trim rhubarb stems before chopping them coarsely

Rub crumble mixture together, using only your fingertips, to avoid melting the butter

apple and rhubarb crumble

PREPARATION TIME **15 minutes** ● COOKING TIME **30 minutes**

SERVES 4

4 medium apples (600g)

20g butter

$^1/_4$ cup (50g) firmly packed brown sugar

$5^1/_2$ cups (600g) coarsely chopped rhubarb

2 tablespoons orange juice

2 cups (60g) corn flakes, crushed slightly

$^1/_2$ cup (35g) shredded coconut

$^1/_3$ cup (75g) firmly packed brown sugar, extra

2 tablespoons plain flour

70g butter, coarsely chopped, extra

1 Preheat oven to moderate.

2 Peel and core apples; cut into thick wedges. Melt butter in large saucepan; cook apple and sugar, stirring, until sugar dissolves and apple just starts to caramelise. Add rhubarb and juice; cook, stirring, until rhubarb is tender. Transfer mixture to 1.5-litre (6-cup) ovenproof dish.

3 Combine corn flakes, coconut, extra sugar and flour in large bowl. Using fingers, rub extra butter into crumble mixture.

4 Spoon crumble mixture evenly over top of apple-rhubarb mixture; bake, uncovered, in moderate oven about 15 minutes or until crumble is golden brown. Serve with scoops of vanilla ice-cream, if desired.

per serving 24.9g fat; 2180kJ

TIPS

● We used granny smith apples in this recipe because their white, firm flesh retains its shape and readily absorbs the butter-sugar mixture when it is cooked. Golden delicious apples are equally as good and can be used for this recipe.

● You'll need to buy a bunch of rhubarb weighing about a kilo in order to get the 600g of chopped stems needed here. The leaves of rhubarb are high in oxalic acid, which can be toxic when eaten in a large quantity, so these and the trimmed bits of top and bottom stem should be discarded.

● Shredded coconut is the dried flesh, sliced into very thin strips. It's best to use this for a crumble rather than the desiccated coconut, which is too fine for the crumble topping.

Mash the banana with the back of a metal fork in a small shallow bowl

Fold banana mixture into the egg white mixture

Run your finger around edge of uncooked soufflés to help them rise evenly

banana soufflés with butterscotch sauce

PREPARATION TIME **20 minutes** ● COOKING TIME **25 minutes**

SERVES 4

1 tablespoon caster sugar

¹/₄ cup (50g) firmly packed brown sugar

2 tablespoons cornflour

¹/₂ cup (125ml) milk

4 eggs, separated

¹/₄ cup mashed banana

2 tablespoons caster sugar, extra

butterscotch sauce

50g butter

¹/₂ cup (100g) firmly packed brown sugar

¹/₂ cup (125ml) thickened cream

1 Preheat oven to moderately hot. Grease four 1¹/₄-cup (310ml) soufflé dishes. Sprinkle bases and sides with caster sugar; shake off excess.

2 Blend brown sugar and cornflour with a little of the milk in small saucepan; blend in remaining milk. Stir over heat until mixture boils and thickens.

3 Combine egg yolks and banana with brown sugar mixture in large bowl; allow to cool.

4 Beat egg whites in small bowl with electric mixer until soft peaks form; gradually add extra caster sugar, beating until sugar dissolves. Gently fold egg white mixture, in two batches, into cooled banana mixture.

5 Spoon soufflé mixture into prepared dishes; smooth tops with rubber spatula. Bake, uncovered, in moderately hot oven about 20 minutes or until soufflés are puffed. Serve immediately with warm butterscotch sauce.

butterscotch sauce Place ingredients in small saucepan. Stir over heat, without boiling, until mixture is smooth.

per serving 28.3g fat; 1939kJ

TIPS

● You need a small overripe banana weighing about 140g for this recipe.

● Separate the individual white and yolk of each egg before combining with those of another to ensure freshness. Eggs separate easier if cracked after they reach room temperature.

● Use spotlessly clean beaters; any trace of grease will prevent egg whites from rising to the required volume. For the same reason, when separating eggs, make sure no yolk taints the white.

● The butterscotch sauce can be made in a microwave oven.

SERVING SUGGESTION
Serve accompanied with thick cream and sliced banana. These rich and absolutely scrumptious soufflés complement our Pork with Orange Mustard Sauce (page 54).

glossary

aioli a garlic mayonnaise.

allspice also known as pimento or jamaican pepper; available whole or ground.

artichoke hearts centre of the globe artichoke; sold in cans or loose, in brine.

bacon rashers also known as bacon slices; made from cured, smoked pork side.

beans
BORLOTTI also known as roman beans; pale pink or beige beans with darker red spots. Eaten fresh or dried; also available in cans.
BROAD also known as fava beans. Available fresh, canned and frozen; best peeled twice (discard outer long green pod and the sandy-green inner shell).
BUTTER also known as lima beans; sold dried and in cans; large, beige, mild-tasting bean.
CANNELLINI small white beans.

bean sprouts also known as bean shoots; tender new growths of beans and seeds germinated for consumption.

beetroot also known as beets.

blue-eye also known as deep-sea trevalla or trevally and blue-eye cod; thick, moist white-fleshed fish.

black mustard seeds also known as brown mustard seeds.

bok choy also called pak choi or chinese white cabbage; has a fresh, mild mustard taste. Baby bok choy is also available.

breadcrumbs
PACKAGED fine-textured, crunchy, purchased, white breadcrumbs.
STALE 1- or 2-day-old bread made into crumbs by grating, blending or processing.

burghul also known as bulghur wheat; hulled steamed wheat kernels that, once dried, are crushed into various-sized grains.

brioche French sweet bread made with egg, butter and yeast; available in many forms.

broccolini a cross between broccoli and chinese kale but milder and sweeter; is completely edible from flower to stem.

butter use salted or unsalted ("sweet") butter; 125g is equal to one stick of butter.

buttermilk fresh low-fat milk cultured to give a slightly sour, tangy taste; low-fat yogurt can be substituted.

caperberries fruit formed after the caper buds have flowered; sold pickled.

capers the grey-green buds of a warm climate shrub sold either dried and salted or pickled in vinegar brine.

capsicum also known as pepper or bell pepper.

carambola also called star fruit or five-cornered fruit; has sweet, white flesh.

cardamom available in pod, seed or ground form; has a distinctive, aromatic flavour.

cashews slightly sweet nuts, native to Brazil. We used unsalted roasted cashews.

cayenne pepper long, hot red chilli; usually purchased dried and ground.

celeriac tuberous root with brown skin, white flesh and a celery-like flavour.

cheese
BOCCONCINI small rounds of fresh "baby" mozzarella; a delicate, semi-soft, white cheese. Spoils rapidly; keep refrigerated, in brine, for 1 or 2 days only.
BRIE buttery soft cheese with an edible, white-mould rind; originally from France. Very high fat content; when ready to eat, a piece of brie should have a quite runny centre.
CHEDDAR the most common cow milk "tasty" cheese; should be aged and hard.
FETTA a crumbly textured goat- or sheep-milk cheese with a sharp, salty taste.
FONTINA Italian in origin; has a brown or red rind. It is semi-hard with a nutty flavour and a few holes.
MASCARPONE a fresh, thick, triple-cream cheese with a delicately sweet, slightly sour taste.

MOZZARELLA a semi-soft cheese with a delicate, fresh taste; has low melting point and stringy texture when hot.
PARMESAN a sharp-tasting, dry, hard cheese, made from skim or part-skim milk and aged for at least a year.
RICOTTA a sweet, fairly moist, fresh curd cheese having a low fat content.

chickpeas also called garbanzos, hummus or channa; an irregularly round, sandy-coloured legume.

chilli available in many types and sizes, both fresh and dried. The smaller the chilli, the hotter it is. Wear rubber gloves when handling chillies, as they can burn your skin. Removing seeds and membranes lessens the heat level.
JALAPEÑO sold finely chopped or whole, bottled in vinegar, as well as fresh.
SWEET CHILLI SAUCE sweet, mild sauce made from red chillies, sugar, garlic and white wine vinegar.

chinese barbecued pork also known as char siew; has a sweet-sticky coating of soy sauce, sherry, five-spice and hoisin sauce. Available from Asian food stores.

chives related to the onion and leek, with subtle onion flavour.
GARLIC have flat leaves and a stronger flavour than chives.

ciabatta meaning "slipper" in Italian, the traditional shape of this popular crisp-crusted white bread.

coconut
CREAM available in cans and cartons; made from coconut and water.
DESICCATED unsweetened, concentrated, dried shredded coconut.
MILK pure unsweetened coconut milk available in cans.

corella pear small, crisp pear having a distinctive pink blush.

coriander also known as cilantro or chinese parsley; leafy green herb with a pungent flavour.

cos lettuce also known as romaine lettuce. Also baby cos.

couscous a fine, grain-like cereal product; made from semolina.

crème fraîche a mature fermented cream (minimum fat content 35%) velvety texture and tangy taste.

curly endive also known as frisée; green salad vegetable with ragged leaves and a slightly bitter flavour.

eggplant also known as aubergine.

fennel also known as finocchio or anise.

fish fillets boned and skinned fish pieces.

fish sauce also called nam pla or nuoc nam; made from pulverised salted fermented fish, most often anchovies.

five-spice powder a fragrant mixture of ground cinnamon, cloves, star anise, sichuan pepper and fennel seeds.

flathead also known as sand or slimy flathead.

flat-leaf parsley also known as continental or italian parsley.

garam masala a blend of roasted and ground spices; originating in North India.

ghee clarified butter, with the milk solids removed; can be heated to a high temperature without burning.

green peppercorns soft, unripe berry of the pepper plant; sold packed in brine.

hoisin sauce a thick, sweet and spicy Chinese paste made from soy beans, onions and garlic.

honeycomb a confection made of sugar, bicarb soda and glucose; available plain or chocolate coated.

horseradish cream paste of grated horseradish, vinegar, oil and sugar.

kaffir lime leaves aromatic leaves of a small citrus tree.

kalamata olives small, brine-cured black olives.

kecap manis Indonesian sweet, thick soy sauce.

kipfler potato small with a nutty flavour; finger-shaped.

kumara orange-fleshed sweet potato.

lamb's lettuce also known as mâche, lamb's tongue or corn salad; clusters of tiny, tender, nutty-tasting leaves.

lebanese cucumber also known as the european or burpless cucumber.

lemon grass a tall, lemon-smelling and -tasting grass; use the white lower stem.

lemon thyme herb with tiny, green citrus-flavoured leaves.

lentils also known as dhal; dried pulse available in brown and red varieties.

maple-flavoured syrup also known as golden or pancake syrup. It is not a substitute for pure maple syrup.

mesclun a mixture of assorted green leaves.

mizuna a wispy, feathered green salad leaf.

mushrooms
BUTTON small, cultivated white mushrooms.
SWISS BROWN also known as cremini or roman; brown mushrooms with full-bodied flavour. Substitute button or cup mushrooms.
FLAT large soft mushrooms with a rich earthy flavour.
OYSTER (abalone) grey-white mushroom shaped like a fan.
SHIITAKE available dried; soak to re-hydrate before use.

mussels they must be tightly closed when bought, indicating they are alive; discard any shells that do not open after cooking.

mustard
DIJON a pale brown, fairly mild French mustard.
SEEDED also known as wholegrain; a coarse-grain mustard made from crushed mustard seeds.

noodles
CRISPY FRIED NOODLES sold packaged already deep-fried and ready to eat; sometimes labelled crunchy noodles.
HOKKIEN also known as stir-fry noodles; fresh wheat-flour yellow-brown noodles.
RICE STICK flat, dried noodles made from rice flour; available thin or wide.

onion
GREEN also known as scallion or (incorrectly) shallot; an onion picked before the bulb has formed. Has long, green, edible stalk.
RED also known as spanish, red spanish or bermuda.
SPRING has green-leafed top and large, sweet, white bulb.

oyster sauce rich sauce made from oysters and brine.

parsnip root vegetable with sweet, ivory flesh.

pine nuts also known as pignoli; small, cream kernels from the cones of several types of pine tree.

pumpkin also known as squash; a member of the gourd family.

risoni small rice-shaped pasta; very similar to orzo.

pide also known as turkish bread; wheat-flour bread available in long flat loaves and individual rounds.

pitta also known as lebanese bread; wheat-flour bread sold in large, flat pieces that separate into two thin rounds.

polenta a cereal made of ground corn (maize); finer and lighter than cornmeal. Also the name of the dish made from it.

prosciutto salt-cured, air-dried, pressed ham; sold in thin slices, ready to eat.

radicchio also known as red chicory, a vegetable with reddish purple leaves and a mildly bitter flavour.

rambutan related to the lychee; tropical fruit covered with red "hair". The flesh is white, juicy and sweet.

ready-rolled pastry quiche, puff or shortcrust pastry; manufactured and sold, under refrigeration or frozen, in sheets or rounds.

red curry paste combination of dried red chillies, onions, garlic, oil, shrimp paste, lemon rind, ground cumin, paprika, ground turmeric and ground black pepper.

rice
ARBORIO plump, round grain, well suited to absorb a large amount of liquid.

BASMATI a white, fragrant long-grain; wash before use.

rice paper also known as banh trang. Made from rice paste and stamped into rounds. Brittle but, dipped briefly in water, becomes a pliable wrapper for food.

rocket also known as rugula, arugula and rucola; a peppery-tasting green leaf.

saffron stigma of a crocus; comes in strands or ground form. Imparts yellow colour to food; store in the freezer.

sambal oelek (also ulek or olek) a salty paste made from ground chillies.

sesame oil made from roasted white sesame seeds; used for flavour, not as a cooking medium.

shrimp paste also known as trasi and blachan; almost solid preserved paste made of salted dried shrimp.

sichuan peppercorns small reddish-brown peppercorn with sharp, aromatic flavour.

snow peas also called mange tout ("eat all"). Snow pea tendrils are sold by greengrocers.

spinach also known as english spinach and, incorrectly, silverbeet; has tender green leaves. Baby spinach is even more tender.

star anise dried star-shaped fruit of tree native to China. The pods have an aniseed flavour and are available whole and ground.

sugar
CASTER also known as superfine or finely granulated table sugar.
ICING also known as icing sugar mixture and confectioner's or powdered sugar.

tarragon a fragrant, distinctively sweet herb.

tabasco sauce brand name of extremely fiery sauce made from vinegar, red peppers and salt.

tahini rich, buttery paste made from sesame seeds.

tamarind concentrate a thick, purple-black, ready-to-use paste extracted from tamarind-bean pulp.

tofu also known as bean curd; made from the "milk" of crushed soy beans. Comes fresh as soft or firm, and processed as fried or pressed dried sheets. Refrigerate leftover fresh tofu in water (changed daily) up to 4 days.
BEAN CURD POUCHES bean curd (tofu) pockets which are opened to take a filling.

tomato
CHERRY also known as tiny tim or tom thumb tomato.
EGG also called plum or roma; oval-shaped tomato.
SUN-DRIED we used sun-dried tomato packed in oil, unless otherwise specified.
TEARDROP small, yellow pear-shaped tomatoes.

tortilla unleavened, round bread; can be purchased frozen, fresh or vacuum-packed. Available made from wheat flour and corn.

turmeric a root that is dried and ground, resulting in pungent, yellow powder.

vietnamese mint narrow-leafed, pungent herb; also known as cambodian mint and laksa leaf.

vine leaves we used vine leaves in brine.

vinegar
BROWN MALT made from fermented malt and beech.
BALSAMIC from Modena, Italy; made from a regional wine of white trebbiano grapes processed then aged in antique wooden casks.
RICE WINE also known as seasoned rice vinegar; made from fermented rice, sugar and salt.

violet crumble bars chocolate-dipped honeycomb.

witlof also known as chicory or belgian endive; pale-green leafed vegetable.

wonton wrappers gow gee, egg or spring roll pastry sheets can be substituted.

worcestershire sauce thin, dark-brown spicy sauce used as a seasoning.

zucchini also known as courgette.

index

measures

One Australian metric measuring cup holds approximately 250ml, one Australian metric tablespoon holds 20ml, one Australian metric teaspoon holds 5ml.

The difference between one country's measuring cups and another's is within a two- or three-teaspoon variance, and will not affect your cooking results. North America, New Zealand and the United Kingdom use a 15ml tablespoon.

All cup and spoon measurements are level. The most accurate way of measuring dry ingredients is to weigh them. When measuring liquids, use a clear glass or plastic jug with the metric markings.

We use large eggs with an average weight of 60g.

dry measures

METRIC	IMPERIAL
15g	½oz
30g	1oz
60g	2oz
90g	3oz
125g	4oz (¼lb)
155g	5oz
185g	6oz
220g	7oz
250g	8oz (½lb)
280g	9oz
315g	10oz
345g	11oz
375g	12oz (¾lb)
410g	13oz
440g	14oz
470g	15oz
500g	16oz (1lb)
750g	24oz (1½lb)
1kg	32oz (2lb)

liquid measures

METRIC	IMPERIAL
30ml	1 fluid oz
60ml	2 fluid oz
100ml	3 fluid oz
125ml	4 fluid oz
150ml	5 fluid oz (¼ pint/1 gill)
190ml	6 fluid oz
250ml	8 fluid oz
300ml	10 fluid oz (½ pint)
500ml	16 fluid oz
600ml	20 fluid oz (1 pint)
1000ml (1 litre)	1¾ pints

length measures

METRIC	IMPERIAL
3mm	⅛in
6mm	¼in
1cm	½in
2cm	¾in
2.5cm	1in
5cm	2in
6cm	2½in
8cm	3in
10cm	4in
13cm	5in
15cm	6in
18cm	7in
20cm	8in
23cm	9in
25cm	10in
28cm	11in
30cm	12in (1ft)

oven temperatures

These oven temperatures are only a guide for conventional ovens. For fan-forced ovens, check the manufacturer's manual.

	°C (CELSIUS)	°F (FAHRENHEIT)	GAS MARK
Very slow	120	250	½
Slow	150	275-300	1 2
Moderately slow	160	325	3
Moderate	180	350-375	4-5
Moderately hot	200	400	6
Hot	220	425-450	7-8
Very hot	240	475	9

ARE YOU MISSING SOME OF THE WORLD'S FAVOURITE COOKBOOKS?

The Australian Women's Weekly Cookbooks are available from bookshops, cookshops, supermarkets and other stores all over the world. You can also buy direct from the publisher, using the order form below.

TITLE	RRP	QTY	TITLE	RRP	QTY
Asian Meals in Minutes	£6.99		Great Lamb Cookbook	£6.99	
Babies & Toddlers Good Food	£6.99		Greek Cooking Class	£6.99	
Barbecue Meals In Minutes	£6.99		Healthy Heart Cookbook	£6.99	
Basic Cooking Class	£6.99		Indian Cooking Class	£6.99	
Beginners Cooking Class	£6.99		Japanese Cooking Class	£6.99	
Beginners Simple Meals	£6.99		Kids' Birthday Cakes	£6.99	
Beginners Thai	£6.99		Kids Cooking	£6.99	
Best Food	£6.99		Lean Food	£6.99	
Best Food Desserts	£6.99		Low-carb, Low-fat	£6.99	
Best Food Fast	£6.99		Low-fat Feasts	£6.99	
Best Food Mains	£6.99		Low-fat Food For Life	£6.99	
Cakes, Biscuits & Slices	£6.99		Low-fat Meals in Minutes	£6.99	
Cakes Cooking Class	£6.99		Main Course Salads	£6.99	
Caribbean Cooking	£6.99		Middle Eastern Cooking Class	£6.99	
Casseroles	£6.99		Midweek Meals in Minutes	£6.99	
Chicken	£6.99		Muffins, Scones & Breads	£6.99	
Chicken Meals in Minutes	£6.99		New Casseroles	£6.99	
Chinese Cooking Class	£6.99		New Classics	£6.99	
Christmas Cooking	£6.99		New Finger Food	£6.99	
Chocolate	£6.99		Party Food and Drink	£6.99	
Cocktails	£6.99		Pasta Meals in Minutes	£6.99	
Cooking for Friends	£6.99		Potatoes	£6.99	
Creative Cooking on a Budget	£6.99		Salads: Simple, Fast & Fresh	£6.99	
Detox	£6.99		Saucery	£6.99	
Dinner Beef	£6.99		Sauces, Salsas & Dressings	£6.99	
Dinner Lamb	£6.99		Sensational Stir-Fries	£6.99	
Dinner Seafood	£6.99		Short-order Cook	£6.99	
Easy Australian Style	£6.99		Slim	£6.99	
Easy Curry	£6.99		Sweet Old-fashioned Favourites	£6.99	
Easy Spanish-style Cookery	£6.99		Thai Cooking Class	£6.99	
Essential Soup	£6.99		Vegetarian Meals in Minutes	£6.99	
Freezer, Meals from the	£6.99		Vegie Food	£6.99	
French Food, New	£6.99		Weekend Cook	£6.99	
Fresh Food for Babies & Toddlers	£6.99		Wicked Sweet Indulgences	£6.99	
Get Real, Make a Meal	£6.99		Wok Meals in Minutes	£6.99	
Good Food Fast	£6.99		TOTAL COST:	£	

Mr/Mrs/Ms _____

Address _____

_____ Postcode _____

Day time phone _____ Email* (optional) _____

I enclose my cheque/money order for £ _____

or please charge £ _____

to my: ☐ Access ☐ Mastercard ☐ Visa ☐ Diners Club

PLEASE NOTE: WE DO NOT ACCEPT SWITCH OR ELECTRON CARDS

Card number ☐☐☐☐ ☐☐☐☐ ☐☐☐☐ ☐☐☐☐ ☐☐☐☐

Expiry date _____ 3 digit security code (found on reverse of card) _____

Cardholder's name_____ Signature _____

* By including your email address, you consent to receipt of any email regarding this magazine, and other emails which inform you of ACP's other publications, products, services and events, and to promote third party goods and services you may be interested in.

To order: Mail or fax – photocopy or complete the order form above, and send your credit card details or cheque payable to: Australian Consolidated Press (UK), Moulton Park Business Centre, Red House Road, Moulton Park, Northampton NN3 6AQ, phone (+44) (0) 1604 497531 fax (+44) (0) 1604 497533, e-mail books@acpmedia.co.uk or order online at www.acpuk.com
Non-UK residents: We accept the credit cards listed on the coupon, or cheques, drafts or International Money Orders payable in sterling and drawn on a UK bank. Credit card charges are at the exchange rate current at the time of payment.
Postage and packing UK: Add £1.00 per order plus 50p per book.
Postage and packing overseas: Add £2.00 per order plus £1.00 per book.
All pricing current at time of going to press and subject to change/availability.
Offer ends 31.12.2007